CLUE BOOKS

Insects

And Other Small Animals
Without Bony Skeletons

Gwen Allen   Joan Denslow

OXFORD UNIVERSITY PRESS

Oxford University Press, Great Clarendon Street, Oxford OX2 6DP

Oxford New York
Athens Auckland Bangkok Bogotá Bombay
Buenos Aires Calcutta Cape Town Dar es Salaam
Delhi Florence Hong Kong Istanbul Karachi
Kuala Lumpur Madras Madrid Melbourne
Mexico City Nairobi Paris Singapore
Taipei Tokyo Toronto

and associated companies in
Berlin Ibadan

Oxford is a trade mark of Oxford University Press

© Oxford University Press 1997
First published 1970
New edition 1997

CLUE BOOKS - INSECTS and other Small Animals without Bony Skeletons
was produced for Oxford University Press
by Bender Richardson White, Uxbridge

Editors: Lionel Bender, John Stidworthy   Design: Ben White
Media Conversion and Page Make-up: MW Graphics
Project Manager: Kim Richardson
Original artwork: Derek Whiteley
Additional artwork: Ron Hayward, Clive Pritchard

A CIP catalogue record for this book is available from the British Library

ISBN 0-19-910177-9 (hardback)   ISBN 0-19-910188-3 (paperback)

1 3 5 7 9 10 8 6 4 2

Printed in Italy

CONTENTS

ABOUT THIS BOOK

This book is about small land animals without bony skeletons that are common in northern and western Europe. Animals of this kind can be found under stones, in soil, among dead leaves, under the bark of trees, and on the flowers and stems of plants. The book allows you to identify these animals and it tells you a little about their lifestyles and habits. In order to use this book you will need to look at real animals. A magnifying lens will help you to see them more clearly. When you have looked at the living animals, be sure to put them back where you found them.

The book is divided into three main sections: Introduction, Clues and Identification. The Clues section allows you to identify each animal you have found. Start on page 6 and follow the clues. The arrows and numbers in the right-hand margin tell you which page to go to next.

The Identification Section consists of information about each major group of small land animal and double-page colour plates illustrating the individual types or species. Most of the animals you find will be illustrated in this section. Alongside each illustration is a basic description of the animal. Throughout the book, measurements are given in millimetres or centimetres, abbreviated to mm or cm (1 cm = 10 mm = 2/5th inch). On some colour plates, the real size of the animals illustrated is shown by a black line beside each drawing.

The coloured band at the top of each double-page spread helps you locate the relevant sections of the book: *blue* for Introduction, *yellow* for Clues, *red* for Identification. An arrowhead at the top right of a page or spread shows the topic continues on to the next page or spread. A bar at the top right indicates the end of that topic.

All animals without bony skeletons lay eggs.

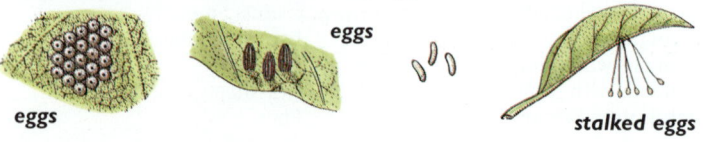

eggs

eggs

stalked eggs

Some eggs hatch into young animals
that do not at first look like their parents.
At this stage of their life they are called
LARVAE. Each larva eats a great deal
of food. It sheds its skin every time
the skin becomes too small.

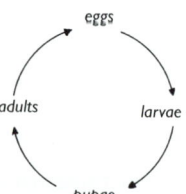

eggs

adults

larvae

pupae

larvae

When the larva is full grown it changes into a **PUPA** and later becomes
an **ADULT**.

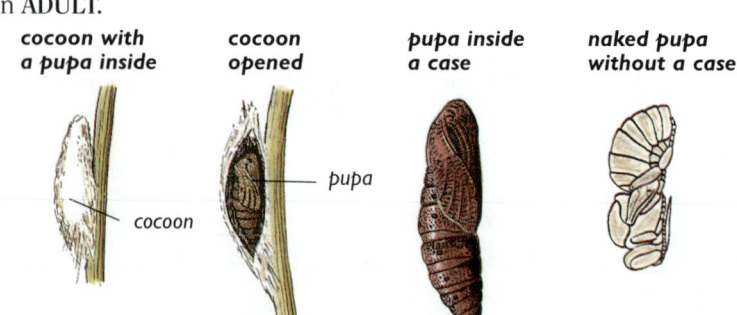

**cocoon with
a pupa inside**

**cocoon
opened**

**pupa inside
a case**

**naked pupa
without a case**

—— pupa

cocoon

Some eggs hatch into young animals that look rather like their parents, except that they have no proper wings. These animals are called **NYMPHS**.

wing bud

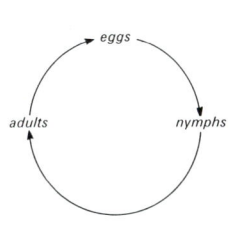

after moulting

Each nymph eats a great deal of food. It sheds its skin every time the skin gets too small for it. After each moult the wings are seen to be bigger.

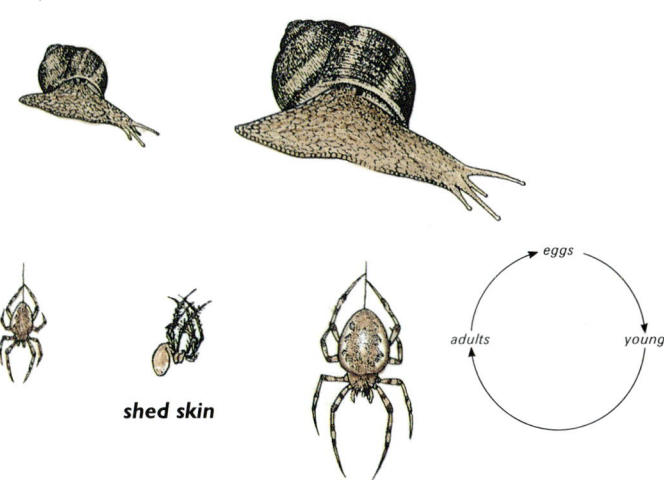

shed skin

Some eggs hatch into young that look exactly like their parents, and some grow without shedding their skins.

CLUES TO NAMING LAND ANIMALS WITHOUT BONY SKELETONS

Most of the parts of animals drawn to illustrate the clues are larger than life size.

CLUE A   If it has wings, six jointed legs and three parts to its body (head, thorax and abdomen), it is an **INSECT**.

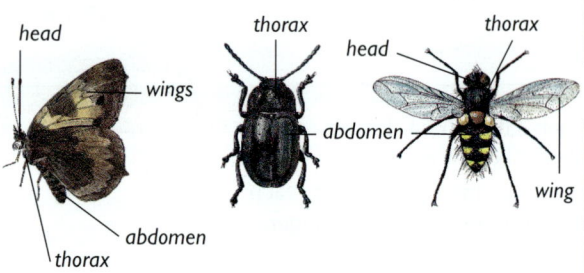

CLUE B   If it has no wings, six jointed legs and three parts to its body (head, thorax and abdomen), it is an **INSECT**.

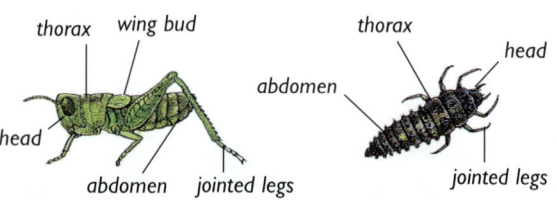

LUE C | If it has six jointed legs, some sucker feet and no wings, it is an insect larva called a **CATERPILLAR.** 15

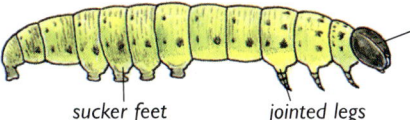

head

sucker feet *jointed legs*

LUE D | If it has no wings, eight jointed legs and only one or two parts to its body, it belongs to the **SPIDER** group (ARACHNIDS). 16

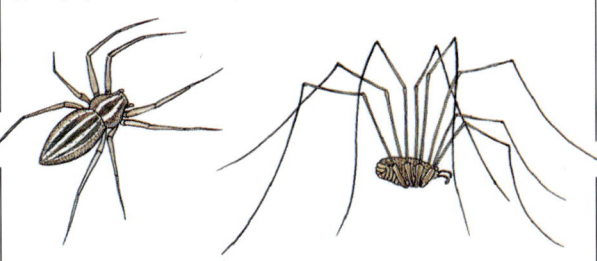

CLUE E | If it has many jointed legs and no wings, it is a **CENTIPEDE, MILLIPEDE** or **WOODLOUSE.** 17

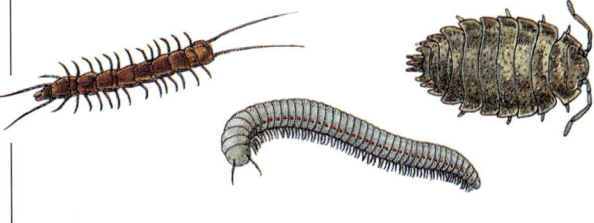

CLUE F | If it has no legs and no wings 18

Look carefully at the wings of the animal.

CLUE A If the animal has two pairs of wings with **POWDERY** scales

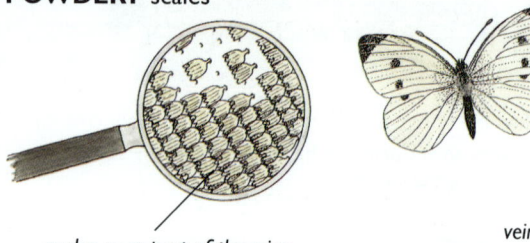

scales on a part of the wing

veins

CLUE B If the animal has two pairs of transparent wings with veins

CLUE C If the animal has two pairs of wings in which the upper wing forms a hard cover and the lower wings are transparent

CLUE D If the animal appears to have only one pair of wings

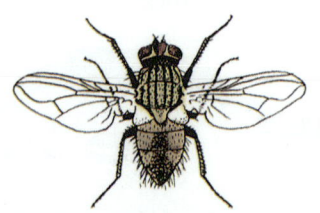

Look carefully at its feelers. These are called
antennae.

LUE A

If the antennae have a club-shaped end, the animal is a
BUTTERFLY (Lepidoptera).

 20

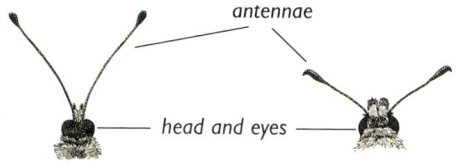

antennae

head and eyes

LUE B

If the antennae are without a club and look rather
feathery, like this

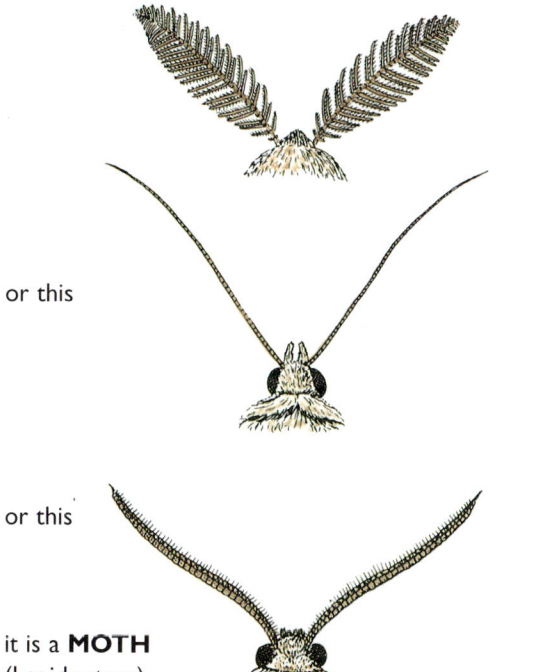

or this

or this

it is a **MOTH**
(Lepidoptera).

 26

CLUE A

Look carefully at the hard wing cases.

If the hard wing cases cover most of the body, the animal belongs to the **BEETLE** group (Coleoptera).

If it has hard wing cases and a shield-like part (scutellum) on its back, the animal is a **FROG-HOPPER** or other **BUG** (Hemiptera).

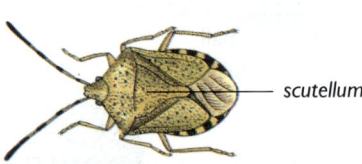

scutellum

If the wings are longer than the horny cases and the animal has very long hind legs, it belongs to the **GRASSHOPPER** group (Orthoptera).

If the hard wing cases cover the wings and are shorter than the body, and if the animal has a pair of pincers at the end of the abdomen, it is an **EARWIG** (Dermaptera).

If the hard wing cases are shorter than the body but there are no pincers, and if the animal rears its abdomen when disturbed, it is a **DEVIL'S COACH-HORSE BEETLE** or some other **ROVE BEETLE** (Coleoptera).

 54

CLUE B

This group of true flies with one pair of wings may be mistaken for bees or wasps. If you use a magnifying lens you will see that there are always two small balancing organs, called **HALTERES,** in place of hind wings.

If the animal has a body that is almost as thick as it is long, often covered with thick bristly hairs, it belongs to the group of **SHORT-HORNED FLIES**.

 64

halteres

If the animal has a humped thorax, slender abdomen and is small, it belongs to the group of **MIDGES** and **MOSQUITOES** (Gnats).

 64

halteres

If the animal has a humped thorax, a slender abdomen, long legs and is large, it is a **CRANE-FLY** (Daddy-long-legs).

 64

CLUE A | If the animal has no sign of wings and an abdomen with a very small waist, it is an adult **ANT**.

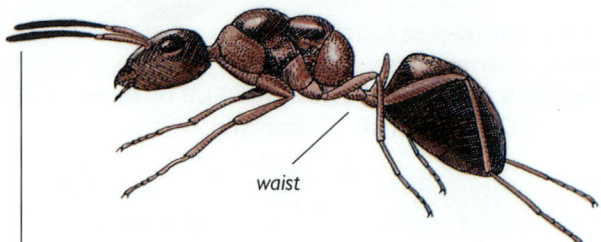

waist

Note that during the summer, you may see swarms of winged ants.

CLUE B | If the animal has no sign of wings, and if its abdomen has no waist, it is either an **APHID**

or a young insect called a **LARVA**.

CLUE C | If the animal has small wing buds, it is a young insect called a **NYMPH**. (Beware, an earwig's hard wing cases may be mistaken for wing buds; see page 8.)

Using a magnifying glass, look carefully at the caterpillar's feet.

CLUE A If the animal has five pairs of sucker feet, ALL with hooks, it is the **LARVA** of a **BUTTERFLY** or **MOTH**.

 20, 26

sucker feet

sucker foot

CLUE B If the animal has only two pairs of sucker feet with hooks, it is a **LOOPER CATERPILLAR,** the larva of a **MOTH**.

 31, 32, 33

CLUE C If the animal has from six to eight pairs of sucker feet, with no hooks, it is a **SAWFLY LARVA**.

 4, 43

sucker foot

Look carefully at the body of the animal.

CLUE A   If the animal has two parts to its body, with the legs attached to the front part, it is a **SPIDER**.

 6

CLUE B   If the animal has only one part to its body it may be either a **HARVESTMAN,** if it has very long legs, or a **MITE** if it is very small (1–4 mm).

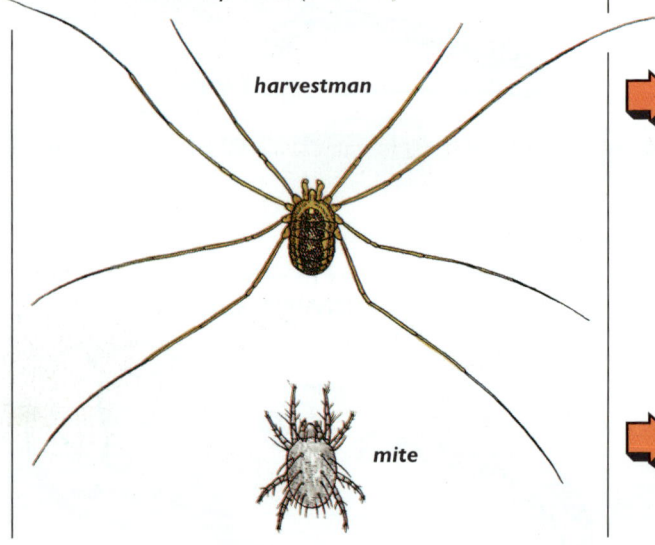

harvestman

mite

70

7

6

CLUE A If the animal has an oval-shaped body with less than fifteen rings, called **SEGMENTS,** and appears to have similar legs on most of them, it is a **WOODLOUSE.**

one segment

72

CLUE B If the animal has a long slender body with more than fifteen segments, and has one pair of long jointed legs on each segment of its body, it is a **CENTIPEDE.**

72

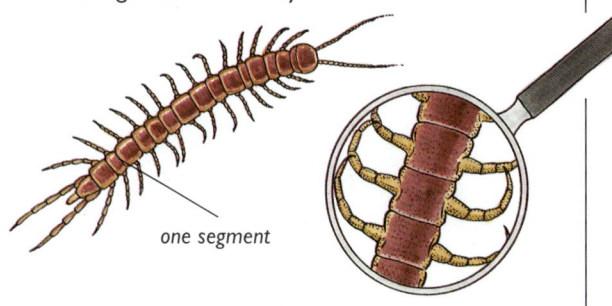

one segment

CLUE C If the animal has a long slender body with more than fifteen segments, and has two pairs of small jointed legs on each segment of its body, it is a **MILLEPEDE.**

73

one segment

CLUE A | If the animal has a shell, two pairs of tentacles and a slimy foot, it is a **SNAIL.**

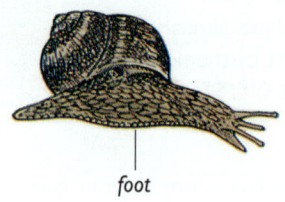

foot

CLUE B | If the animal has no shell, two pairs of tentacles and a flat slimy foot, it is a **SLUG.**

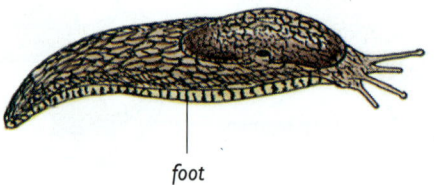

foot

CLUE C | If the animal has no shell, and the body is made up of thirteen or fewer rings, called segments, it is an insect **LARVA** (see page 4).

3
38, 42
6

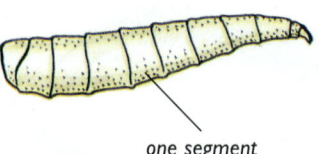

one segment

CLUE D

If the animal has no shell, and the body is made up of more than 100 rings, called segments, it is an **EARTHWORM**.

 73

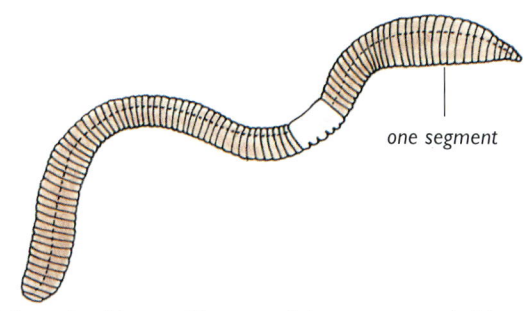

one segment

CLUE E

If the animal is not like any of these, it is probably an insect pupa (see page 4).

Keep your pupa in a box with damp peat to see what it turns into.

adult butterfly emerging from pupa

BUTTERFLIES may be seen in spring and summer. The butterfly feeds on nectar which it sucks from flowers, using the proboscis (a long tube) which is coiled up like a spring beneath its head when not in use. Most butterflies lay their eggs on the plants that the caterpillars will feed on when they hatch (see page 4).

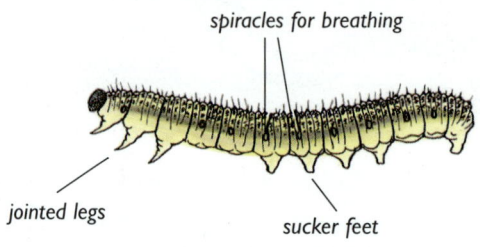

spiracles for breathing

jointed legs

sucker feet

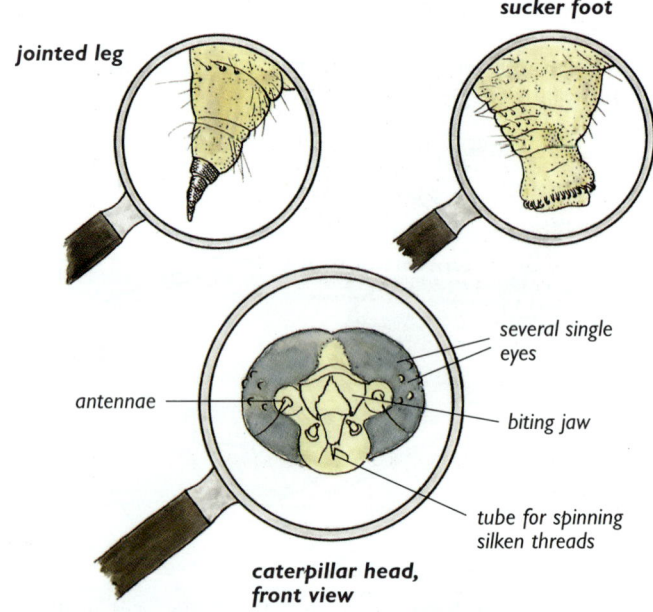

sucker foot

jointed leg

several single
eyes

antennae

biting jaw

tube for spinning
silken threads

**caterpillar head,
front view**

knobbed antennae

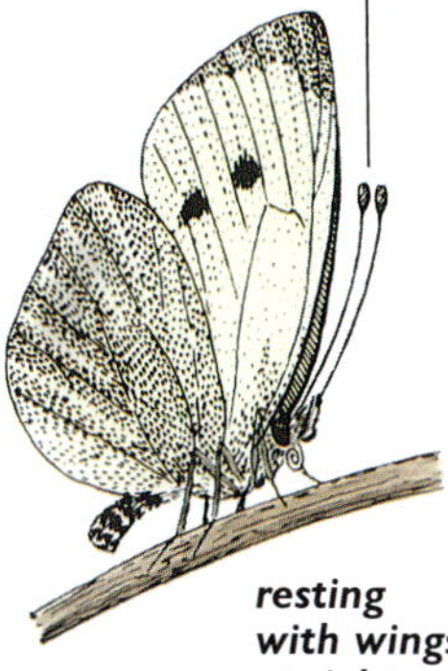

antennae

**resting
with wings
upright**

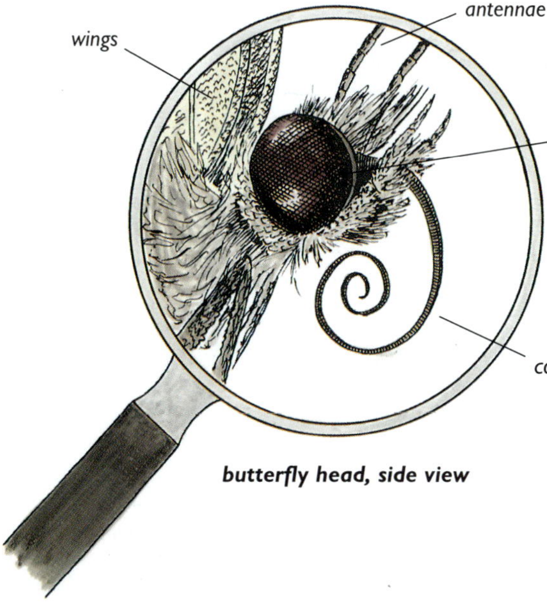

wings

antennae

compound eye
made of many
single eyes

coiled proboscis

butterfly head, side view

If the butterfly you have found is a common one, you will be able to
name it by looking at the illustrations on pages 22–25. If it is more
rare you will need to look at a butterfly book (see page 80).

female

pupa

male

larva

Common Blue
(Wingspan 35 mm). Grassy places. Seen May–Sept. Larva feeds on bird's-foot trefoil.

larva

Dingy Skipper
(Wingspan 29 mm). Open rough grassy places. Moth-like. Sexes similar. Seen May–June. Larva feeds on bird's-foot trefoil.

pupa

larva

Ringlet
(Wingspan 50 mm). Tall grass in open or in woodland clearings. Sexes similar. Seen July–Aug. Larva feeds on grasses.

larva

larva

pupa

Dark Green Fritillary
(Wingspan 65 mm). Grassy country, open woods. Fast strong flier. Green scales on silver-spotted hind underwing. Seen Jul–Aug. Larva feeds on violets.

Dark Green Fritillary

Wall Brown
(Wingspan 45 mm). Sunny open places. Basks with wings open. Seen May–June, July–August. Larva feeds on coarse grasses.

Small Heath
(Wingspan 35 mm). Grassy places. Closes wings when settled. Seen June–July, Aug–Sept. Larva eats fine-leaved grasses.

Wall Brown

Small Heath

pupa

larva

larva

larva

pupa

pupa

Meadow Brown

female

male

Meadow Brown
(Wingspan 55 mm). Grassy places. Seen June–Sept. Larva feeds on grasses.

Small Tortoiseshell
(Wingspan 55 mm). Everywhere. Seen spring, Jul, Sept–Oct. Hibernates as adult. Larva feeds on nettles

larva

Red Admiral
(Wingspan 70 mm). Everywhere. Seen Mar– Oct. Larva feeds on nettles

larva

pupa

pupa

Peacock
(Wingspan 68 mm). Flowering banks and gardens. Seen Jul–Sept, then Mar–May after hibernation. Larva feeds on nettles.

larva

larva

pupa

female (male has black only on tips of wings)

Large White
(Wingspan 65 mm). Cabbage fields, vegetable gardens. Seen May–June, Aug. Larva feeds on cabbages and other plants of this family.

pupa

Small White

(Wingspan 48 mm). Everywhere. Agricultural pest. Seen Apr–June, Aug–Sept.

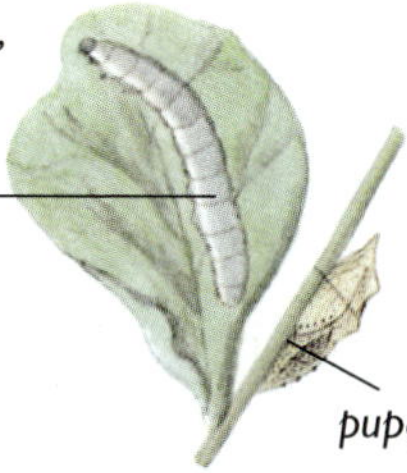

Larva feeds on cabbages, nasturtium, hedgerow weeds

pupa

Green Veined White

(Wingspan 50 mm). Marshy meadows, damp hedgerows. Seen Apr–June, Jul–Sept.

Larva feeds on garlic mustard, water cress and similar plants

pupa

female

pupa

Brimstone

(Wingspan 60 mm). Hedgerows, woodlands. Seen Aug until hibernation, then early spring–May.

Larva feeds on buckthorn

male

From pages
9, 15

INTRODUCING MOTHS

MOTHS may be seen from spring until the frosts come in autumn. Some of them feed on nectar which they gather from night-scented flowers. Most moths fly at night and rest with their wings spread. They lay their eggs on the plants that the caterpillars will eat when they hatch (see page 4).

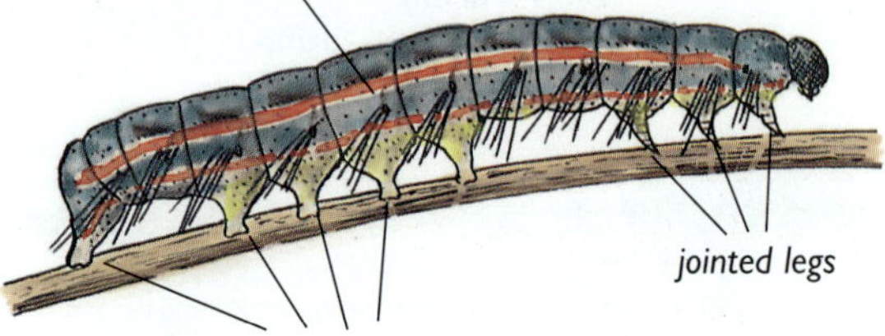
spiracle
jointed legs
sucker feet

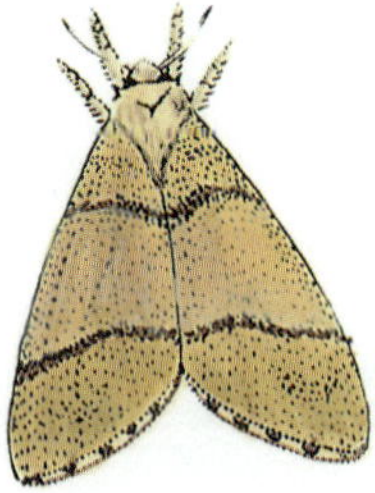
resting with
wings together

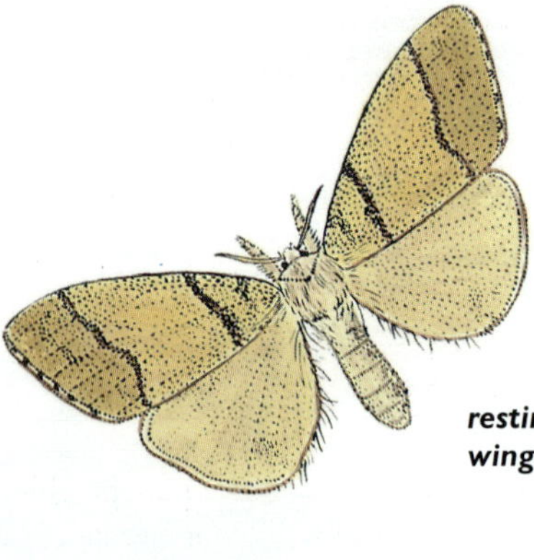
resting with
wings spread

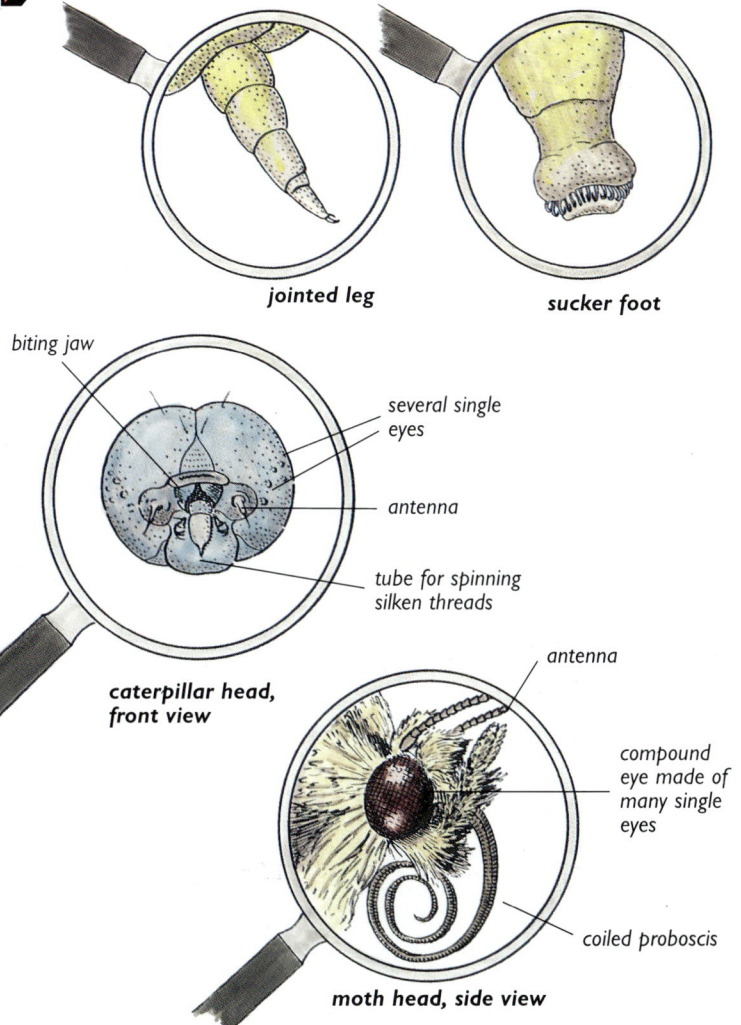

jointed leg

sucker foot

biting jaw

several single
eyes

antenna

tube for spinning
silken threads

**caterpillar head,
front view**

antenna

compound
eye made of
many single
eyes

coiled proboscis

moth head, side view

If the moth you have found is a common one, you may be able to
name it, or its group, by looking at the illustrations on pages 28–33.
As there are hundreds of different kinds of moths you may need to
look in a moth book (see page 80).

Eyed Hawk
(Wingspan 90 mm). Seen June.
Larva feeds on willow
and apple leaves.

larva

Cinnabar
(Wingspan 40 mm). Open dry
country. Seen May–June. Fly by day
as well as dusk. Larva feeds
on ragwort and groundsel.

larva

*pupa (winters
in the soil)*

larva

Privet Hawk
(Wingspan 100 mm). Seen
May–Jul. Larva feeds on
privet, honeysuckle and
lilac.

pupa

larva

Garden Tiger
(Wingspan 60 mm). Seen July–Aug. 'Woolly bear' larva feeds on many plants, especially garden weeds.

pupa in silken cocoon in spring

Lime Hawk
(Wingspan 60 mm). Seen May–June. Larva feeds on lime and elm trees.

Yellow Underwing
(Wingspan 60 mm). Seen June–Oct. Larva feeds on low-growing plants, including garden plants.

Burnet
(Wingspan 30 mm). Downland, open country. Seen flying by day, May–Aug. Larva feeds on bird's-foot trefoil.

larva

larva

cocoon

pupa

Lappet
(Wingspan 60 mm). Hedgerows, woodland edges. Seen June–Aug. Larva feeds on blackthorn, hawthorn and fruit trees in autumn, then hibernates until spring.

larva

cocoon of silk on food plant

Oak Eggar
(Wingspan 55 mm). Heaths, open woods, and near sea. Seen July–Aug. Larva feeds on bramble, heather and hawthorn. Pupa in silken cocoon on the ground.

larva

male

female

Lackey
(Wingspan 35 mm). Seen Jul–Aug.
Larva feeds on hawthorn and other trees.

eggs

larva

larva

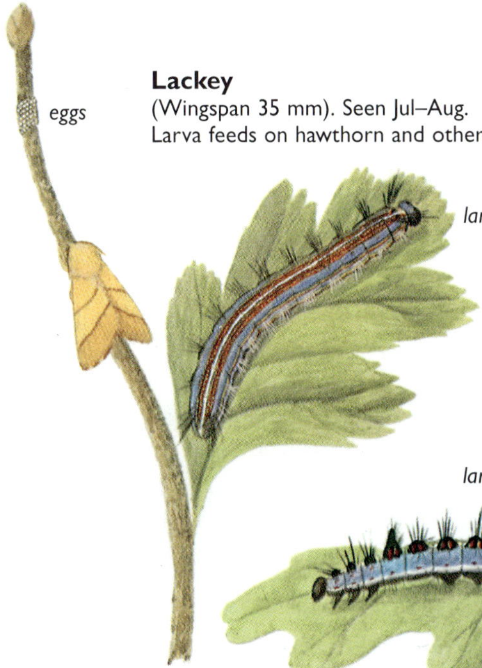

Dagger
(Wingspan 40 mm). Seen
June–July. Larva feeds on lime,
hawthorn and other trees.

Brimstone
(Wingspan 30 mm). Woods,
hedgerows and elsewhere.
Seen Apr–Sept. Larva eats
hawthorn and blackthorn.

*larva
(looper)*

larva

Drinker
(Wingspan 50 mm). Damp open country. Seen July. Larva feeds on coarse grasses and drinks the rain droplets.

Garden Carpet
(Wingspan 25 mm). Seen Apr–Oct. Larva feeds on cabbage and other plants of the cabbage family.

larva (looper)

larva

Puss Moth (Wingspan 55 mm).
Seen May–June. Larva feeds on willow and poplar. Cocoon of silk and chewed wood on tree bark.

Early Thorn
(Wingspan 40 mm). Seen Apr–May, Jul–Aug. Larva feeds on thorn and other trees.

larva (looper)

Wainscot
(Wingspan 40 mm). Seen June–Jul. Larva feeds on grasses and rushes.

larva

Magpie
(Wingspan 40 mm). Seen Jul–Aug. Larva feeds on gooseberry and redcurrant bushes.

larva (looper)

pupa

Buff-Tip
(Wingspan 60 mm). Seen June–Jul. Larva feeds on variety of trees.

larva (looper)

HONEY BEES live in hollow trees or in hives provided by beekeepers. They make combs of six-sided cells with wax, which they scrape from glands underneath their abdomens. Honey is stored and eggs are laid by the queen in different parts of the comb. During the winter the workers and queens live in the hive feeding on the stored honey.

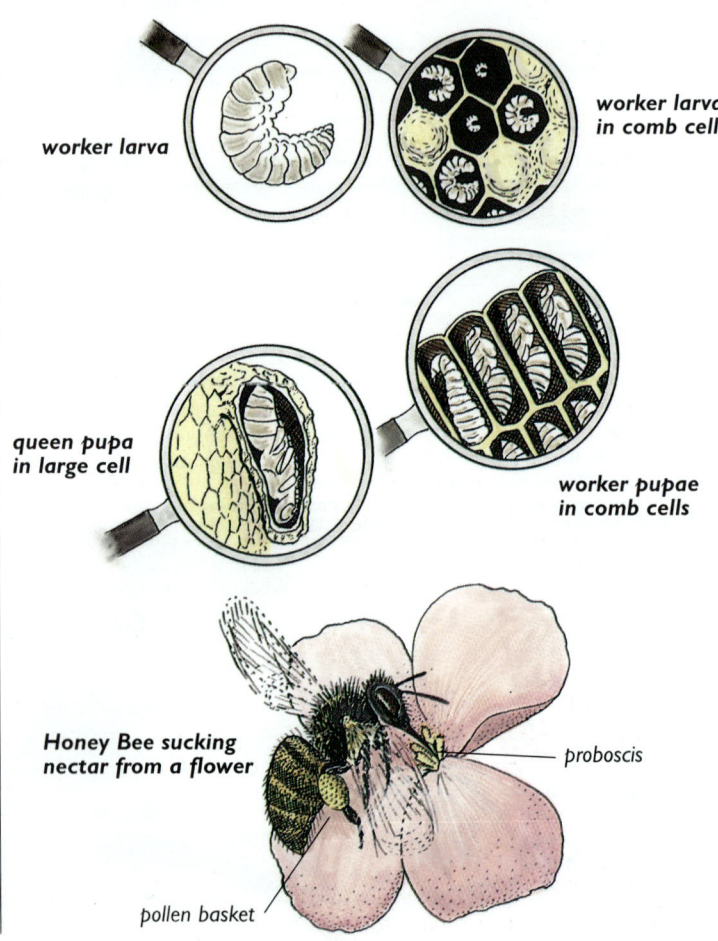

worker larva

worker larvae in comb cells

queen pupa in large cell

worker pupae in comb cells

Honey Bee sucking nectar from a flower

proboscis

pollen basket

The worker bees may be seen from early spring until late autumn gathering nectar and pollen from flowers on sunny days. They use their proboscis (long hollow tube) to collect the nectar. The pollen clings to their hairy bodies and they use their front and hind legs to brush it into pollen baskets on their hind legs (see illustrations below). You can see the proboscis and pollen baskets quite clearly by watching bees visiting flowers on warm, sunny days.

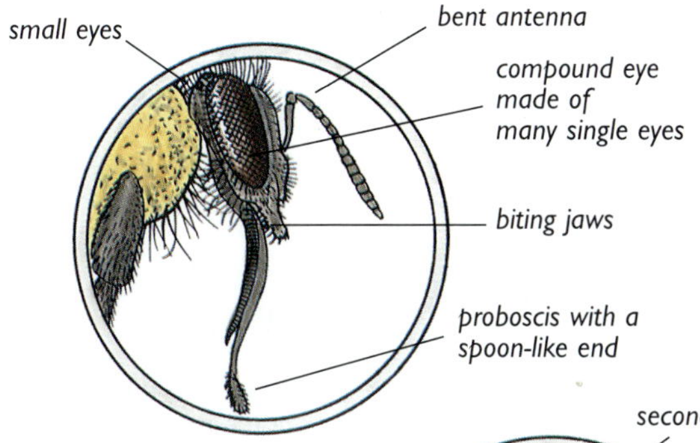

small eyes

bent antenna

compound eye made of many single eyes

biting jaws

proboscis with a spoon-like end

side view of head

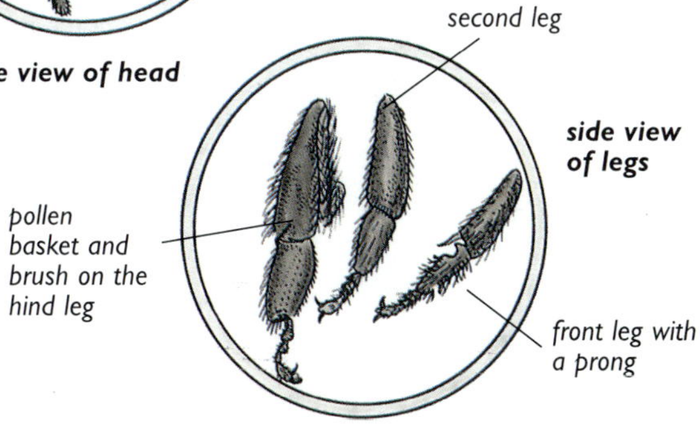

second leg

side view of legs

pollen basket and brush on the hind leg

front leg with a prong

There are many different kinds of bees. If there is no picture on pages 36–37 of the one you have found, you will need to look at a book about bees (see page 80).

BUMBLE BEES. Their nests are made new each year in a hole in a bank or in a crevice by a queen that has overwintered underground. Workers and males die each autumn.

cells

drone

queen

hive bees worker

Honey Bee

(Workers' body length 12 mm). Almost all are domesticated and live in human-made hives, although this species can live wild. The bees store food in the hive and overwinter there.

Early Bumble Bee

(Body length 18 mm). Appears early spring. Nests below ground.

wax cells

Bumble Bee's nest

Buff-tailed Bumble Bee

(Body length 18 mm)

Leaf-cutting Bee
(Body length 14 mm). Cuts
semicircles from leaves such as
roses. Rolls them into cylinders in
which eggs are laid in hole
in wood.

cut leaf

*Leaf-cutting
Bee's nest*

**Large Red-tailed
Bumble Bee**
(Body length 22 mm). Builds
large nests in mouse holes.

WASPS

The queen wasp comes out of hibernation in early spring and begins to build the first cells of the nest. She lays an egg in each of these cells. When the eggs hatch she catches insects to feed the larvae (see life cycle on page 4). In a short time the larvae become pupae and then worker wasps.

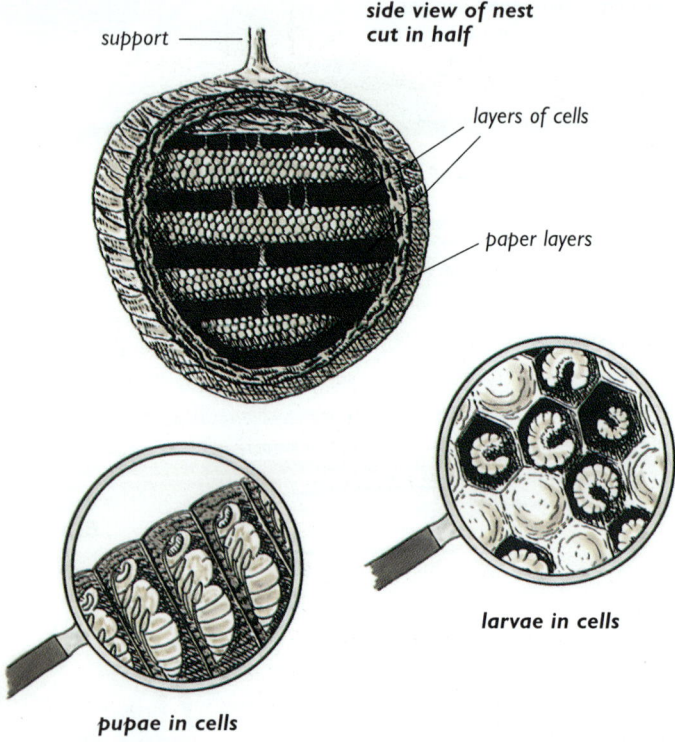

side view of nest cut in half

support

layers of cells

paper layers

larvae in cells

pupae in cells

In summer worker wasps scrape wood to make paper to enlarge the nest; they collect food for new larvae.

The queen continues to lay eggs but takes no further part in nest building or the care of the young. Wasps feed mainly on fruit and other sweet things. In autumn when the frosts come all wasps, except the queen, die.

wings folded against side

compound eye made of many single eyes

bent antennae

sting

biting jaws

worker wasp

SOLITARY WASPS live alone and the females make small nests. Digger wasps build them in holes in the ground. Potter wasps often hang them from plants. The female lays one egg in each cell. She catches and paralyses insects or small animals, which she puts into the cells for the larvae to feed on.

ICHNEUMONS, BRACONIDS AND CHALCIDS

These are parasitic Hymenoptera and lay eggs in insects, particularly caterpillars, on which their larvae feed. When the larvae are full-grown they become pupae; then the insect they have been feeding on dies.

drone

queen

nest

Common Wasp
(Body length: queen 25 mm,
worker 20 mm).

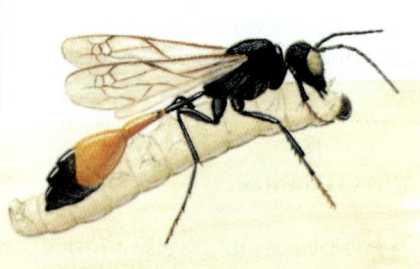

Sand Wasp
(Body length 20 mm).
Sandy heathland areas.
Kills caterpillars to provision
nest-hole.

Digger Wasp
(Body length 15 mm). Makes
vertical burrows in hard sandy
ground. Preys on weevils.

wasp workers

Ichneumon
(Body length 19 mm).
Sometimes flies into houses.
Lays its eggs in moth
caterpillars.

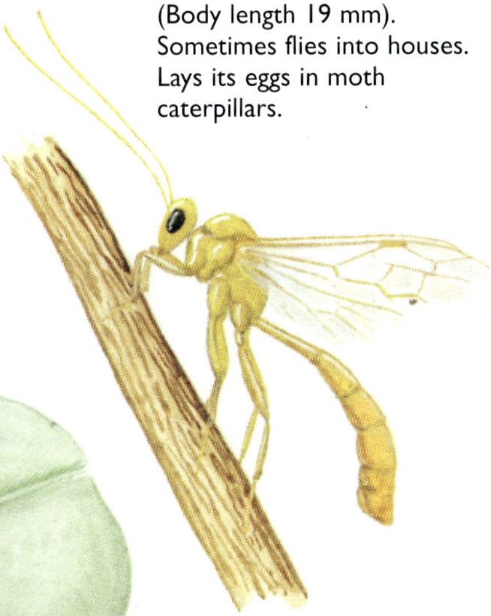

*cocoons of
braconid
on a
caterpillar*

*caterpillar in
which Ichneumon
has laid eggs*

Braconid
(Body length under 3 mm). Lays eggs
in caterpillar of large white butterfly.
Larva feeds on this and then pupates
on the caterpillar's body.

ANTS

Ants live all the year round in the soil of gardens, meadows and woodlands. The queen begins to lay eggs in early spring (see life cycle, page 4). Groups of eggs, larvae and pupae are cared for by worker ants. In late summer on hot sultry days, small winged males and large winged queens fly from the nests in swarms. After mating, the queen returns to the nest and bites off her wings. Ants feed mainly on sweet juices from fruits and from greenflies. They make tracks from the nest, which they follow when foraging.

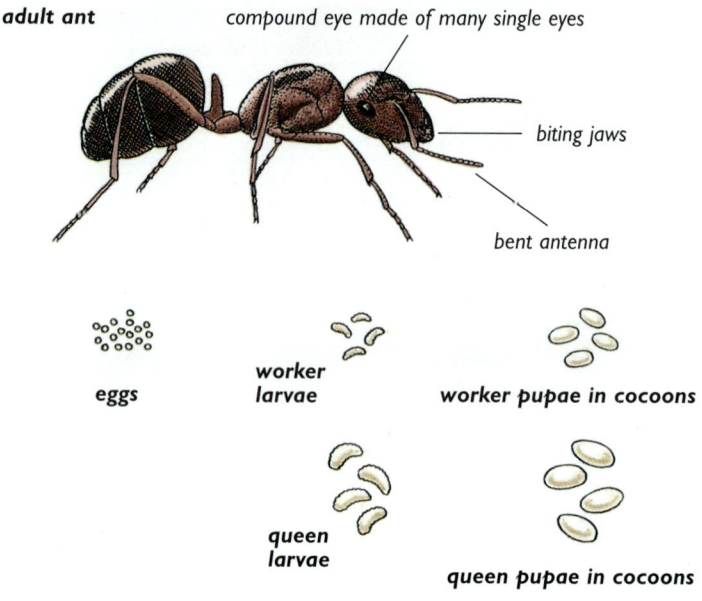

adult ant

compound eye made of many single eyes

biting jaws

bent antenna

eggs

worker larvae

worker pupae in cocoons

queen larvae

queen pupae in cocoons

SAWFLIES

Sawflies have a saw-like tube called an ovipositor through which
they lay their eggs. These they lay in minute holes that they saw in
the stems or leaves of the plants on which the caterpillars will feed
when they hatch (see life cycle, page 4).

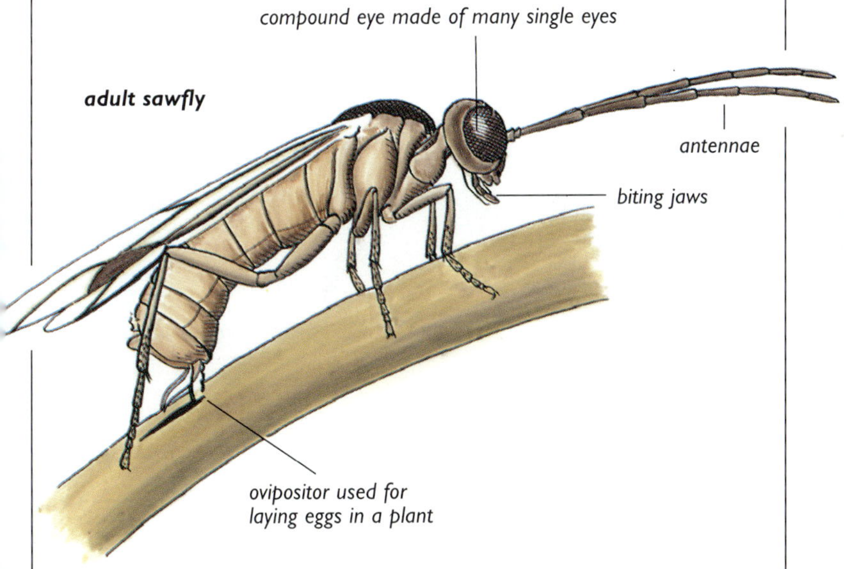

compound eye made of many single eyes

adult sawfly

antennae

biting jaws

*ovipositor used for
laying eggs in a plant*

Red Ant
(Body length: worker 5mm). Nests under
stones. Common in gardens. May sting.

mound

male *queen* *worker*

queen *mound* *worker*

male

Black Ant
(Body length: worker
4 mm, queen 9 mm).
Nests under stones and logs. Often in gardens.
Sometimes invades houses. Swarms in hot weather.

mound

Wood Ant
(Body length: worker 9 mm. Males
and queens larger). Builds domes
of twigs and leaves over the
nest. Often noticeable in
conifer woods.

worker *male* *queen*

larva

Gooseberry Sawfly
(Body length: adult 8 mm). Larva strips leaves of gooseberry and currant bushes.

Hawthorn Sawfly
(Body length: adult 16 mm). Larva feeds on hawthorn. Pupa can be seen on hawthorn in winter.

pupa

Apple Sawfly
(Body length: adult 7 mm). Larva feeds on and spoils developing apple fruit.

larva

pupa

larva

cocoon

The animals shown on this page lay their eggs in water. As the young live in water they are not shown in this book about land animals.

DRAGONFLIES

Dragonflies dart about near water, catching flying insects. They hold the insects between their legs while feeding on them.

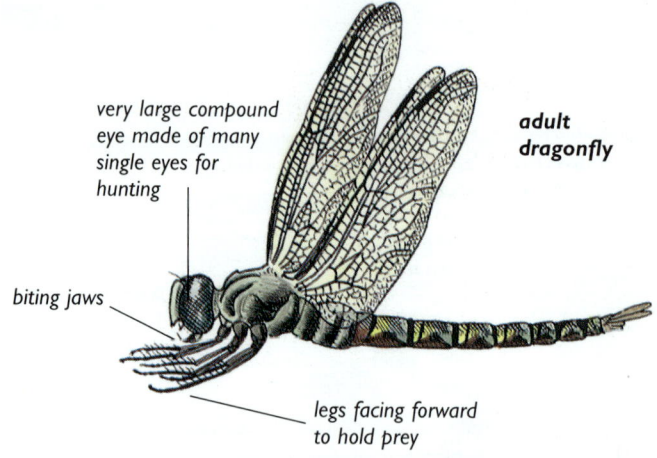

very large compound eye made of many single eyes for hunting

adult dragonfly

biting jaws

legs facing forward to hold prey

ALDERFLIES

Alderflies may be seen resting among plants by streams.

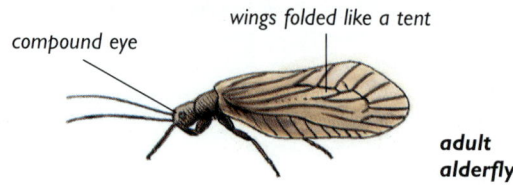

compound eye

wings folded like a tent

adult alderfly

MAYFLIES

Swarms of mayflies dance over the water surface on warm sunny days. The last skin is shed after their first flight. Before this moult fishermen call them 'duns'; afterwards they call them 'spinners'. Adult mayflies live for only a short time because they cannot feed.

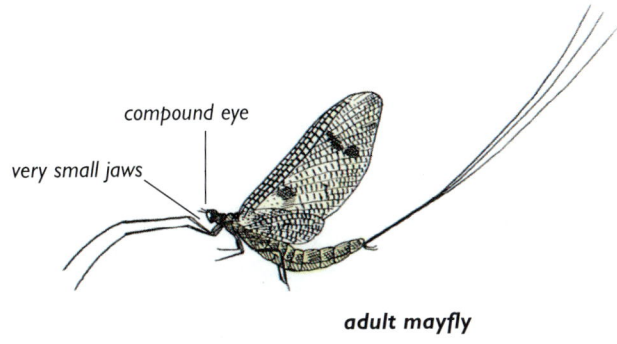

compound eye

very small jaws

adult mayfly

CADDIS-FLIES

Caddis-flies often rest among plants during the day, and usually fly at night. They lick up sweet juices.

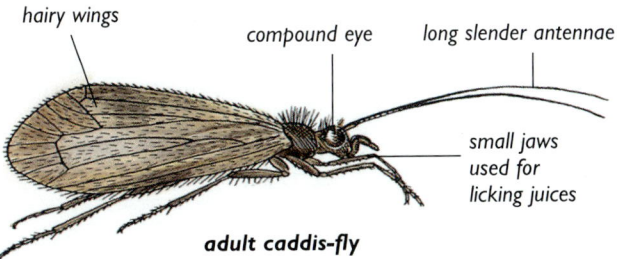

hairy wings

compound eye

long slender antennae

small jaws used for licking juices

adult caddis-fly

Hawker Dragonfly
(Body length 70 mm).
Flies fast and strongly.
Sometimes travels far
from water.

male

**long-bodied
dragonflies**

female

Broad-bodied Dragonfly
(Body length 45 mm). Darts from a
perch to hunt, then returns to it.

Mayfly Duns

female

male

Mayfly Spinners
(Length 40 mm)

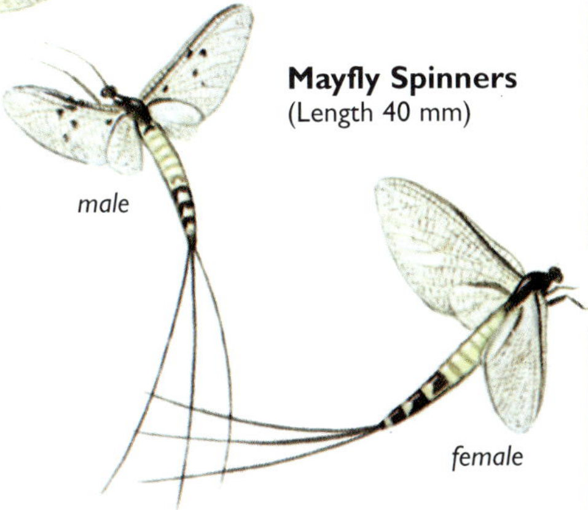

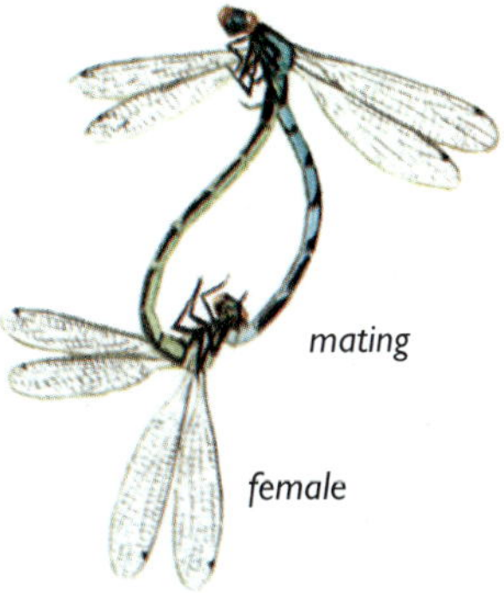

male

male

female

mating

female

Damselfly
(Body length 30 mm).
More delicate than dragonfly.
Folds wings on perching. Like
dragonflies, flies 'in tandem'
when mating.

Alderfly
(Body length 17 mm).
Flies weakly in
late spring. Often
rests on plants.

LACEWINGS

Lacewings live in gardens during the summer. They lay clusters of stalked eggs on the tops of plants on which aphids feed. Both the larvae and the adult lacewings feed on aphids.

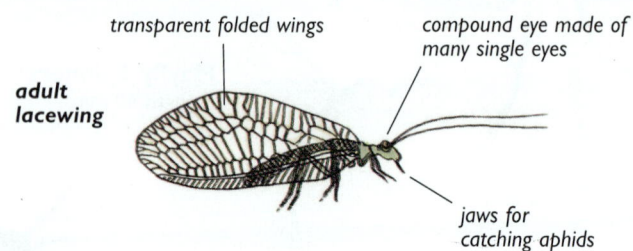

transparent folded wings

compound eye made of many single eyes

adult lacewing

jaws for catching aphids

APHIDS

Aphids may be black, green or white. They pierce plants with their sharp jaws and suck up the juices. Aphids breed very rapidly. Hundreds of them of different ages and sizes may be seen on plants. Most of the aphids are wingless; but the winged ones fly to new food plants and start new colonies.

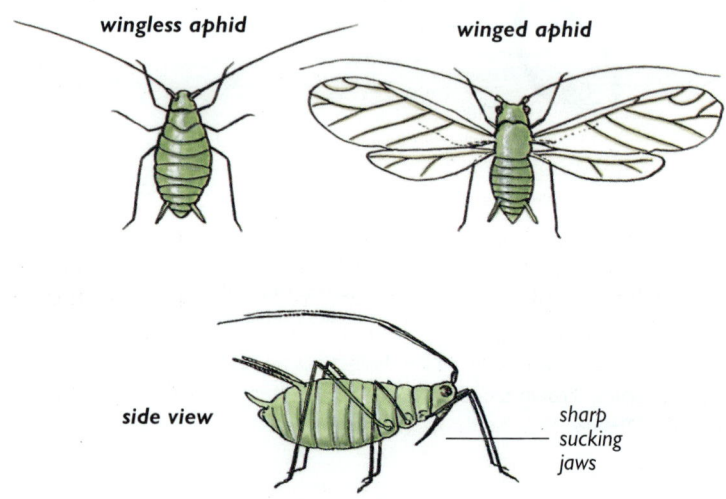

wingless aphid

winged aphid

side view

sharp sucking jaws

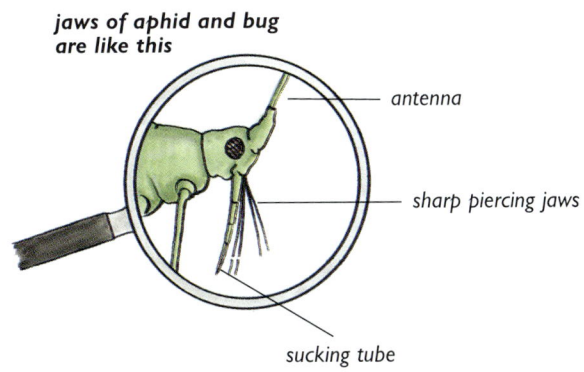

jaws of aphid and bug
are like this

antenna

sharp piercing jaws

sucking tube

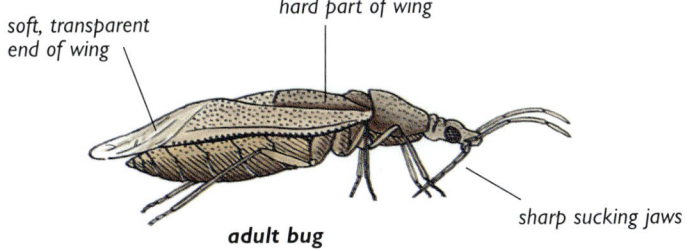

soft, transparent
end of wing

hard part of wing

sharp sucking jaws

adult bug

BUGS

Shieldbugs, capsid bugs and frog-hoppers are the more common
bugs. During the summer adults and nymphs (see life cycle, page 4)
suck juices from plants. Frog-hoppers live in long grass, and hop
when disturbed. The eggs hatch in early spring, and the nymphs
feed on sugary sap from plants. They also use the sap to make
'cuckoo spit', a frothy white substance that protects the growing
nymph. Most frog-hoppers mature in June.

stalked eggs

larva covered with debris

larva

Woolly Aphid
(Body length about 2 mm).
Feeds on trees, especially
apple. Causes round swellings,
and makes fluffy white
substance that can
cover colonies.

Green Lacewing
(Body length 15 mm).
Woods, hedgerows, gardens.

Brown Lacewing
In trees and
tall vegetation.

nymph

cuckoo spit

Frog-hopper
(Body length 5 mm).
Nymph in 'cuckoo-spit' during spring.
Adults seen June–Nov.

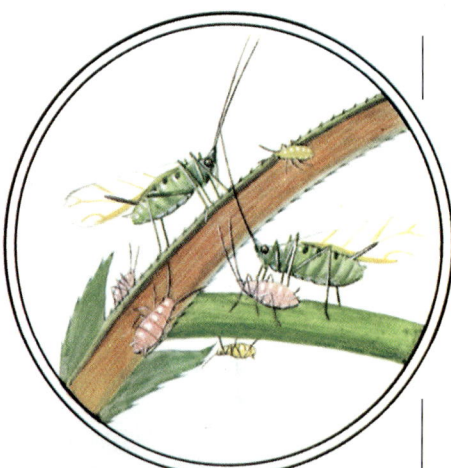

Green Aphid
(Body length about 2 mm).
Often seen on roses in
gardens.

**Black bean
Aphid**
(Body length 2 mm).
Infests beans and other
garden plants in summer.

nymph

Capsid Bug
(Body length 8 mm)

nymph

Shieldbug
(Body length 12 mm). Hard fore-
wings fold over thin hindwings.
Uses stink glands for defence.

BEETLES

Beetles may be found almost anywhere, but more especially under stones and among plants. All beetles have biting jaws; some feed on live animals; some on plants; and others, the scavengers, feed on dead plants and animals.

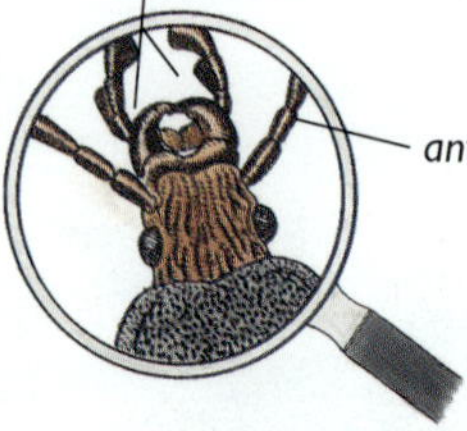

biting jaws

antennae

head

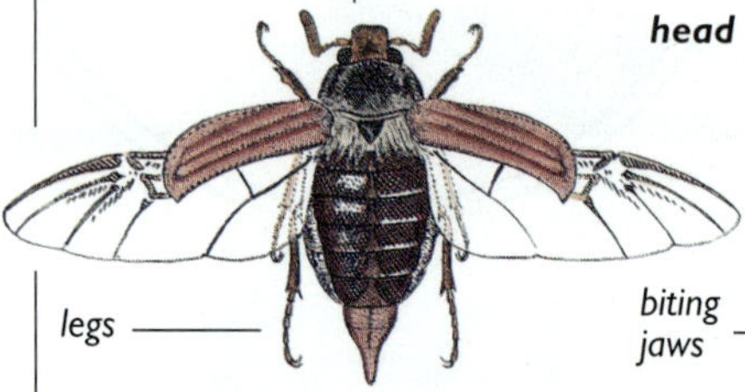

biting jaws

legs

beetle with wings spread

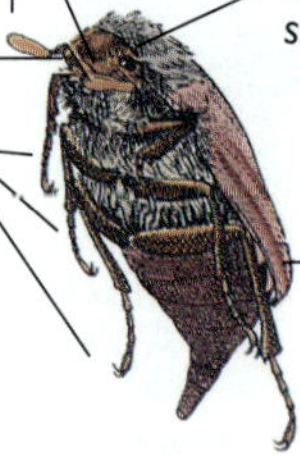

antennae

biting jaws

legs

compound eye made of many single eyes

hard wing

There are hundreds of kinds of beetles. The more common ones have antennae that look like these:

(all are enlarged)

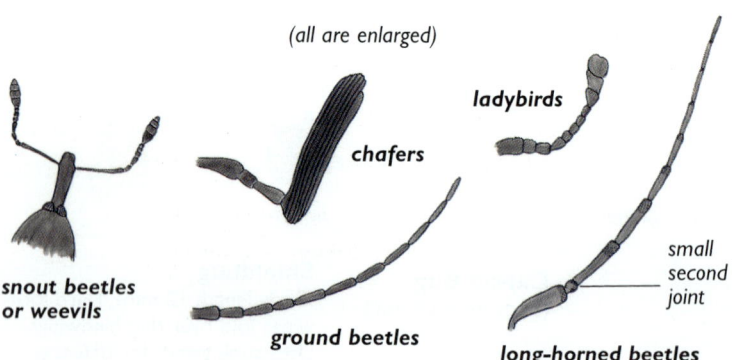

ladybirds

chafers

snout beetles or weevils

ground beetles

small second joint

long-horned beetles

All beetles lay eggs where the larvae will find food when they hatch.
Some larvae hunt for their food; some are fat and soft-bodied and
feed on rotten wood or roots. The larvae usually turn into pupae
underground and so do not need to be protected by a hard covering.

head　　　　**soft-bodied larva** 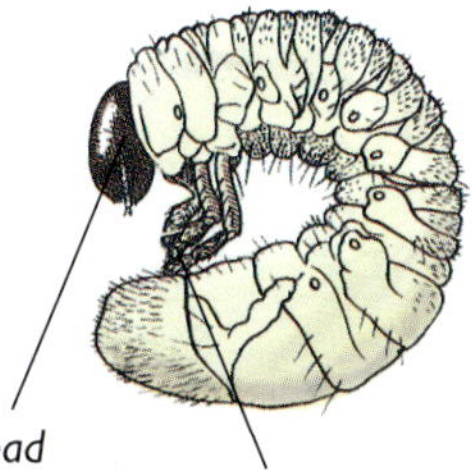　　　**pupa in wood or soil**

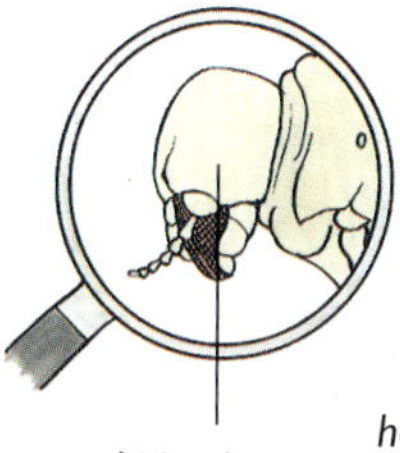

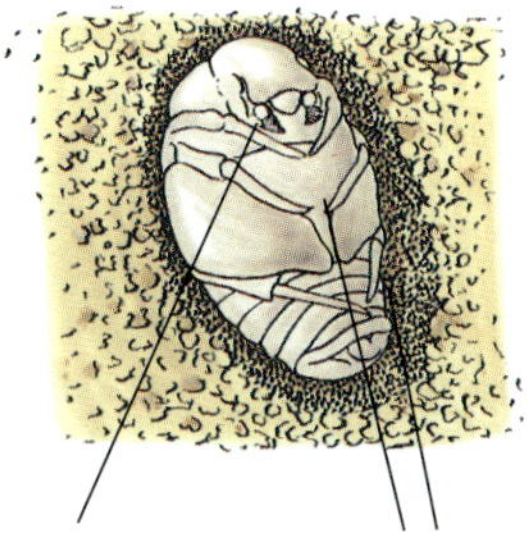

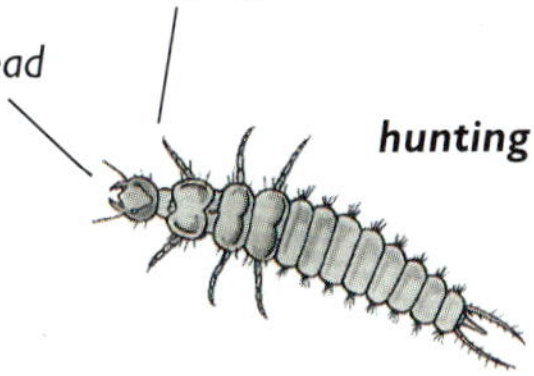

biting jaws

head

short
legs

jaws　　　　legs

long legs

head

hunting larva

**ladybird
pupa
on leaf**

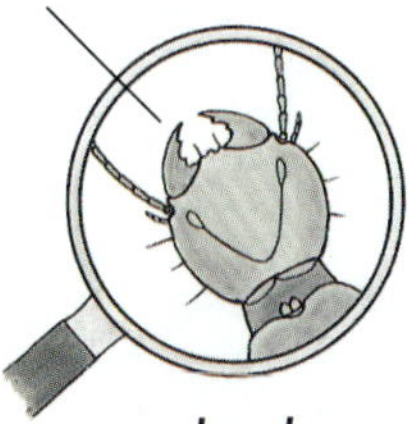

biting jaws

head

pupa in wood or soil

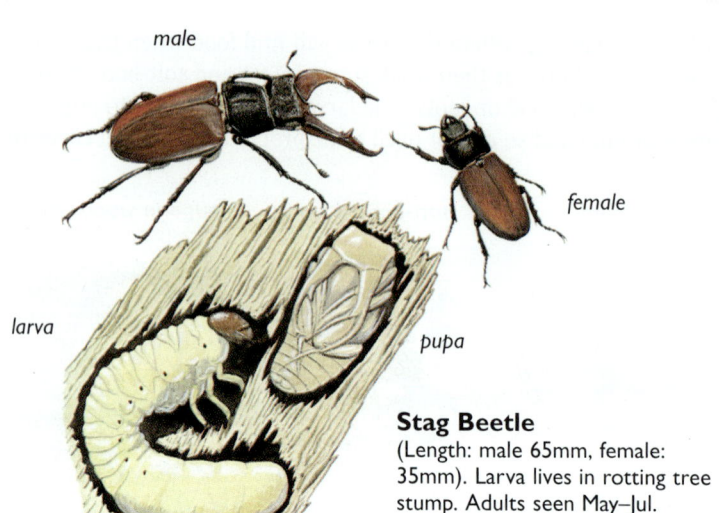

male

female

larva

pupa

Stag Beetle
(Length: male 65mm, female: 35mm). Larva lives in rotting tree stump. Adults seen May–Jul.

Dor Beetle
(Body length 25 mm). Flies on still evenings, with humming flight. Digs burrow under dung to lay eggs. Larva feeds on the dung.

Sexton Beetle
(Body length 20 mm). Buries animal corpse to feed young.

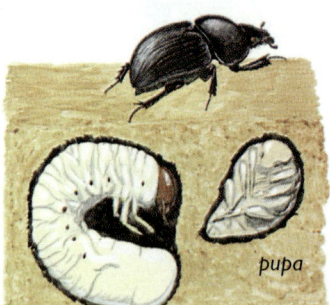

pupa

larva

larva

pup

male

female

Cockchafer
(Body length 25 mm).
Adults feed on tree leaves,
larvae on grass and cereal
roots. Adults fly at dusk and
night in early summer –
sometimes called 'maybug'.

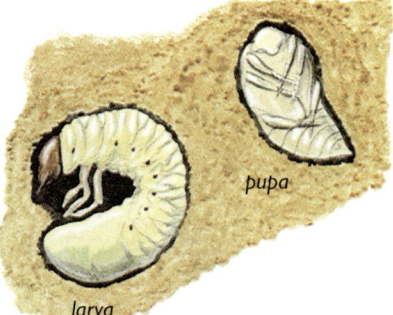

pupa

larva

larva

pupa

Pine Weevil
(Body length 12 mm).
Feeds on buds and young
bark of conifers.

Rose Chafer
(Body length 20 mm).
Seen in early summer, often
sitting on flowers. Larva
feeds on rotting wood.

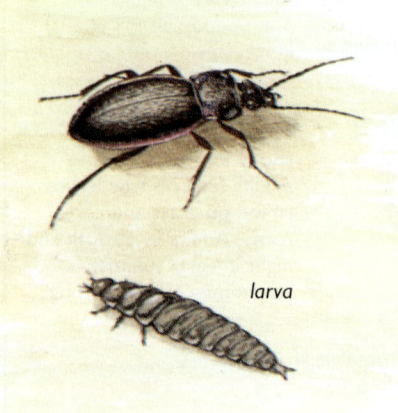

Violet Ground Beetle
(Body length 30 mm). Likes woods and gardens. Flightless. Hunts worms and insects at night, June–Aug. Hides in day.

larva

larva

Rove Beetle
(Body length 5 mm). Lives in decaying matter.

larva

Tiger Beetle
(Body length 14 mm). Mainly in sandy and heathland areas. Active in the sun, Apr–Sept. Run after prey, caught with huge jaws. Larva ambushes prey from burrow.

Devil's Coach-horse
(Body length 30 mm).
Open country, including farmland. Mostly active at night, under stones or bark during day.
Larva and adult fierce predators. Can nip.

larva

Soldier Beetle
(Body length 10 mm).
Often seen on flowers
in summer. Larva lives
on the ground.

7-spot Ladybird
(Body length 7 mm). Adult and larva
eat aphids on low-growing plants.

larva

pupa

larva

Wasp Beetle
(Body length 14 mm).
Found on beech and other
trees May–July. Larva develops
in wood.

larva

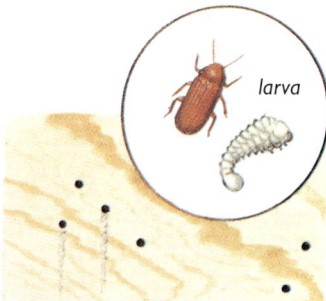

larva

Furniture Beetle
(Body length 5 mm). Larva called
woodworm. Feeds on furniture and
house timbers. Adult gnaws way out
and flies in June and July.

larva

Wireworm
(Body length 10 mm). Larva
eats roots, and is a pest.

GRASSHOPPERS AND CRICKETS

Grasshoppers live among plants, in hedgerows, in long grass and on heathland. They may be heard chirruping on warm sunny days. They make the sound by rubbing their hind legs against the outside edge of their wings. They have very long hind legs and are able to jump long distances. Most grasshoppers feed on plants, though the Great Green Bush-cricket sometimes eats animals.

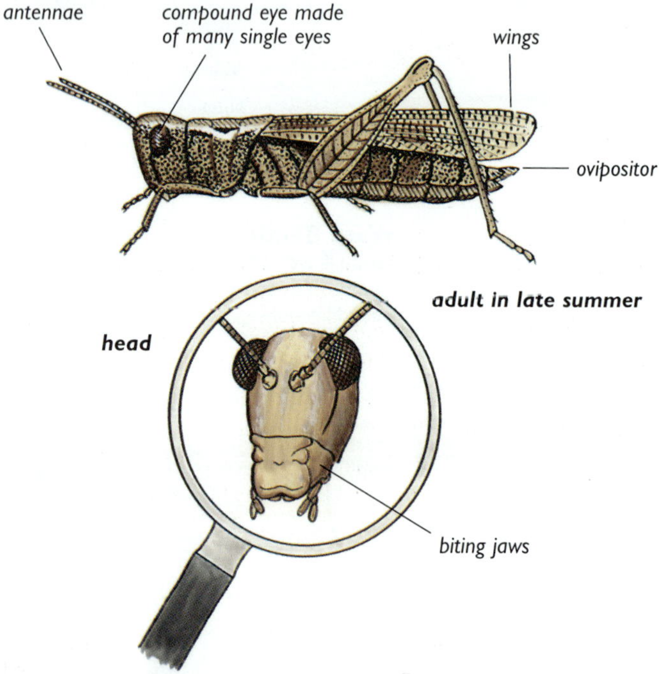

antennae

compound eye made of many single eyes

wings

ovipositor

adult in late summer

head

biting jaws

Crickets are very like grasshoppers but come out at night. House Crickets live in or near buildings.

The Great Green Bush-crickets and Crickets make their chirruping noise by rubbing their wings together.

Grasshoppers lay their eggs at the end of the summer in a hole in the ground which they make with their ovipositor (the tube through which the eggs are laid); then they die. The eggs do not hatch until the following spring.

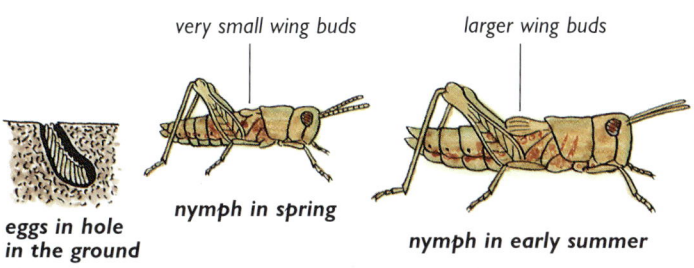

very small wing buds

larger wing buds

**eggs in hole
in the ground**

nymph in spring

nymph in early summer

EARWIGS

Earwigs may be found in flowers, rotten wood, under stones and in other damp dark places. They nibble flower petals but are mainly scavengers (page 54). The female earwig lays eggs in a small hole in the ground or in rotten wood, and then guards them until the nymphs that hatch are old enough to look after themselves.

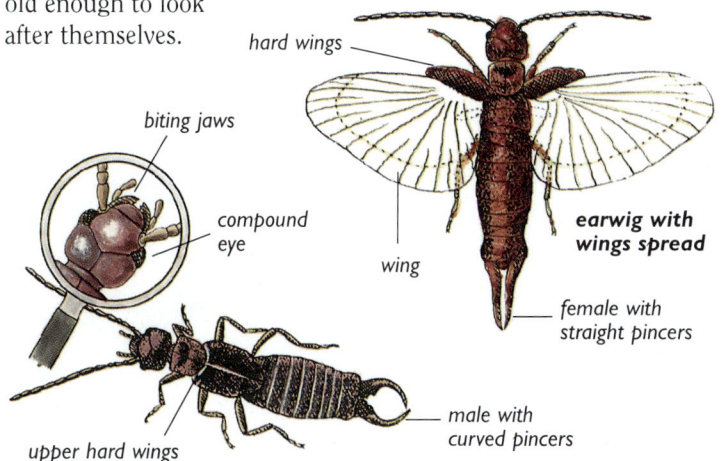

hard wings

biting jaws

compound eye

wing

**earwig with
wings spread**

*female with
straight pincers*

*male with
curved pincers*

upper hard wings

short antennae

Common Green Grasshopper
(Body length 20 mm). Grassy places and moorland. A fast 'ticking' song. June–Oct.

Common Green nymph

House Cricket
(Body length 22 mm). Originally tropical. Mainly an indoor pest in Europe, and on warm rubbish dumps. Shrill chirp.

Field Cricket
(Body length 25 mm). Burrows. Rare in England. In south. Chirps May–Aug.

nymph

Common Field Grasshopper
(Body length 24 mm). Dry open places.
Many together, give chirping song. June–Nov.

short antennae

nymph

Great Green Bush-cricket
(Body length 50 mm). In thick
vegetation. In Britain, in south only.
Loud hissing song.

*very long
antennae*

*Great Green
Bush-cricket
nymph*

male

Earwig
(Body length 15 mm).
In gardens and elsewhere. Nocturnal.
Hides in crevices in day.

female with nymphs

FLIES

Flies suck up juices from decaying plants and animals or nectar from flowers. Midges and mosquitoes (gnats) may suck blood as well. Many hover-flies may be seen on sunny days hovering over flowers or darting from one to the other.

Many flies lay their eggs on the dead plants or animals, which the larvae (maggots) then eat when they hatch.

Hover-fly larvae feed on aphids (see page 50). Crane-flies lay their eggs in grass; the larvae (Leather-jackets) eat the roots.

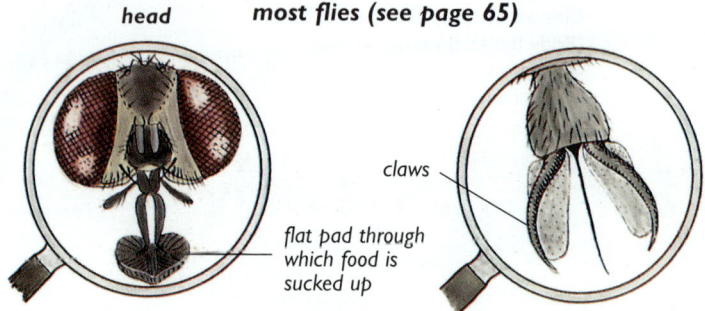

head

most flies (see page 65)

claws

flat pad through
which food is
sucked up

foot with two sucker pads

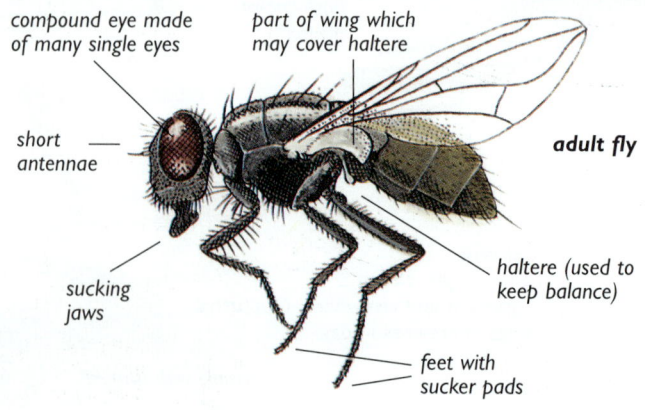

compound eye made
of many single eyes

part of wing which
may cover haltere

short
antennae

adult fly

sucking
jaws

haltere (used to
keep balance)

feet with
sucker pads

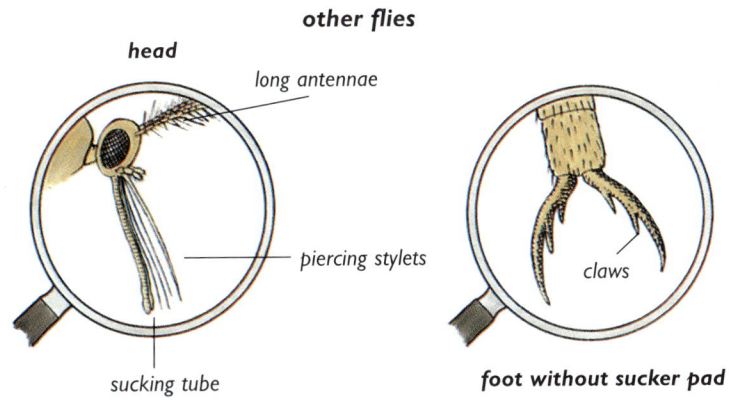

other flies

head

long antennae

piercing stylets

sucking tube

claws

foot without sucker pad

Midges and mosquitoes lay their eggs in water; as the larvae and pupae live in water they are not shown in this book about land animals.

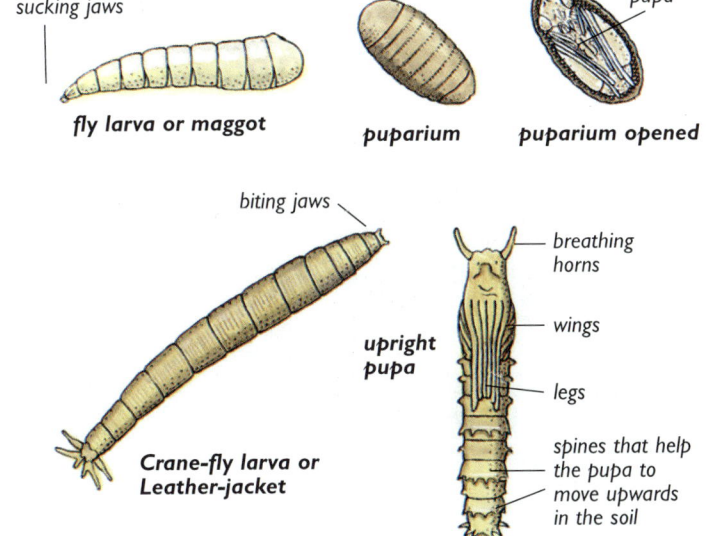

sucking jaws

fly larva or maggot

puparium

pupa

puparium opened

biting jaws

breathing horns

wings

legs

spines that help the pupa to move upwards in the soil

upright pupa

Crane-fly larva or Leather-jacket

House Fly

(Body length 8 mm). Larvae feed
on excrement and decaying matter.
House flies can carry diseases to
our food.

larva

larva

Horse Fly

(Body length 15 mm). Females
are bloodsuckers, may bite
humans. Males drink nectar.
Near cattle, horses, June–Aug.

Hover-fly

(Body length 11 mm).
Adult feeds on nectar
and pollen, Apr–Nov.
Larvae may eat aphids.

larva

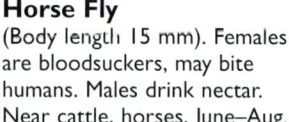

Robber Fly

(Body length 25 mm).
Catches prey with bristled
legs, then piercing mouth-
parts inject poison
before sucking prey
insect dry. Late summer.

larva

larva

Greenbottle
(Body length 10 mm).
In countryside. Lays eggs in dead flesh.

pupa

Bluebottle
(Body length 12 mm). House pest,
sometimes even in winter. Lays eggs
on dead flesh.

larva

pupa

Mosquito
(Body length 5 mm). Males suck
nectar, females suck blood.

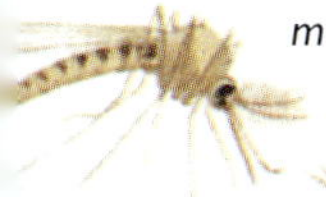

male

male

female

Crane-fly

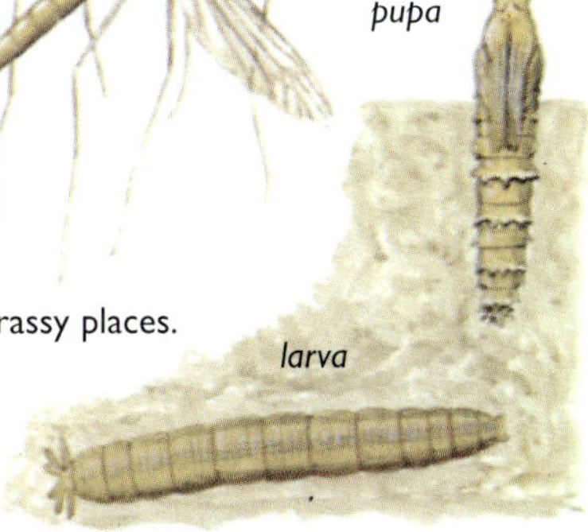

pupa

female

**Crane-fly
(Daddy-long-legs)**
(Body length 40 mm). Grassy places.
Fly at dusk and night.

larva

SPIDERS

Spiders live in buildings, cracks in walls and among plants. They all spin silk and always use a thread as a lifeline when they move from one place to another.

Many spiders use their silk for making webs to catch animals for food. Different groups of spiders have their own particular web shapes (see page 70). When the webs become damaged they have to be mended or remade.

Hunting spiders chase their prey; because they need to see clearly, two of their eyes are very large.

spider seen from below hanging on a web

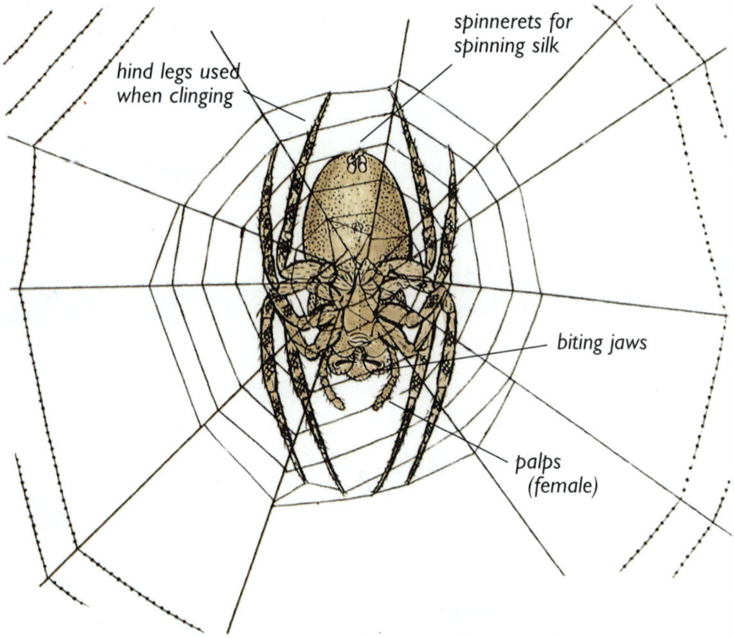

spinnerets for
spinning silk

hind legs used
when clinging

biting jaws

palps
(female)

Spiders lay eggs and wrap them up in silk to form a cocoon. They hatch into tiny spiders (see life cycle, page 5).

large eyes

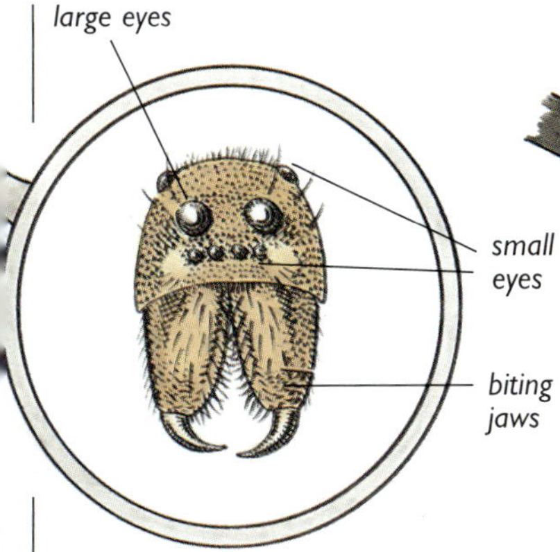

head of male spider

small eyes

biting jaws

eyes

head of hunting spider

large palp (used by male in mating)

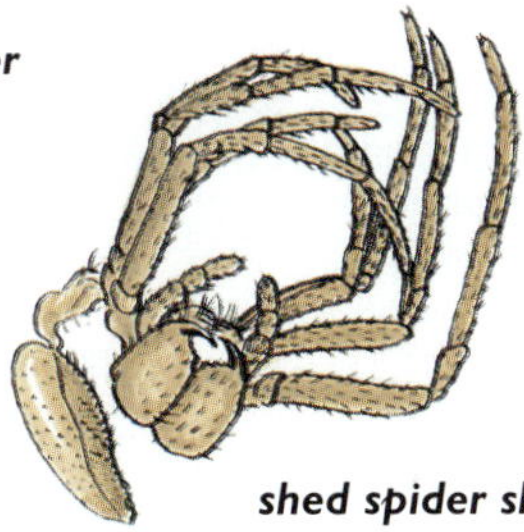

biting jaws

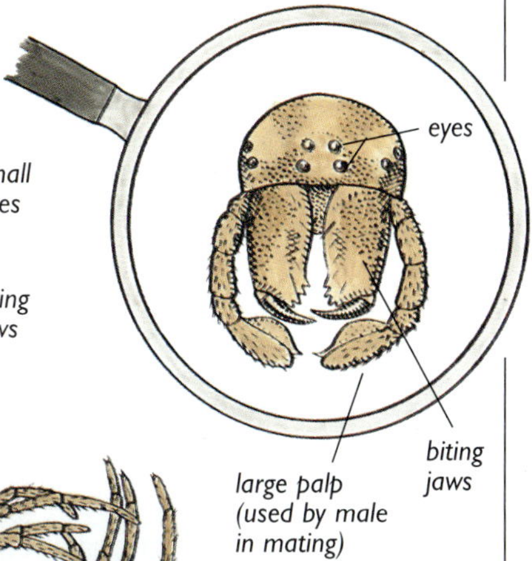

shed spider skin

untidy cocoon of eggs, camouflaged by dust mixed with silk

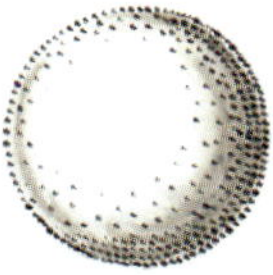

tidy cocoon of eggs

MITES are minute, spider-like creatures. They are numerous, varied, and often pests. RED MITES can be seen on sunny walls. HARVEST MITES are abundant in summer on low vegetation; they can cause skin irritation if they get under tight-fitting clothing.

Linyphia
(Female: 6 mm long, male: 5 mm).
Found almost everywhere. Disperses
by 'parachuting' on a silk strand.
Makes hammock webs with traplines
above. Insects hit lines and fall on
hammock, to be caught by spider
lurking below.

Agelena
(Female: 12 mm long, male: 9 mm).
Builds sheet web with tubular
retreat in bushes. Midsummer.

Theridion
(About 4 mm long). Makes tangled
3-dimensional webs on low plants to
catch flying insects.

Wolf Spider
(Female: 15 mm long, male: 12 mm).
Hunts on ground and on low plants.
Female carries egg-sac under her
body until hatching time.

Harvestman
(Body size about 6 mm). Not a
spider. No venom. No web. Body a
single unit. Feeds on vegetable
matter and small animals. Mainly
seen in autumn. Long thin legs.

Jumping Spider
(Female: 6 mm long, male: 5mm).
Walls, rocks and gardens. Early to
late summer. No web. Stalks prey,
then jumps on it. Excellent eyesight.

orb web

Garden cross spider
(Female: 12 mm long, male:
8 mm). Woods, heaths, gardens.
Late summer, autumn. Orb web
up to 400mm across.

hammock web

Linyphia

Wolf Spider

cocoon

web

Zygiella
(Female: 6 mm long, male: 5 mm).
Near houses, on window frames.
Orb web has 2 missing segments.
Late summer on. May
survive and build web
in winter.

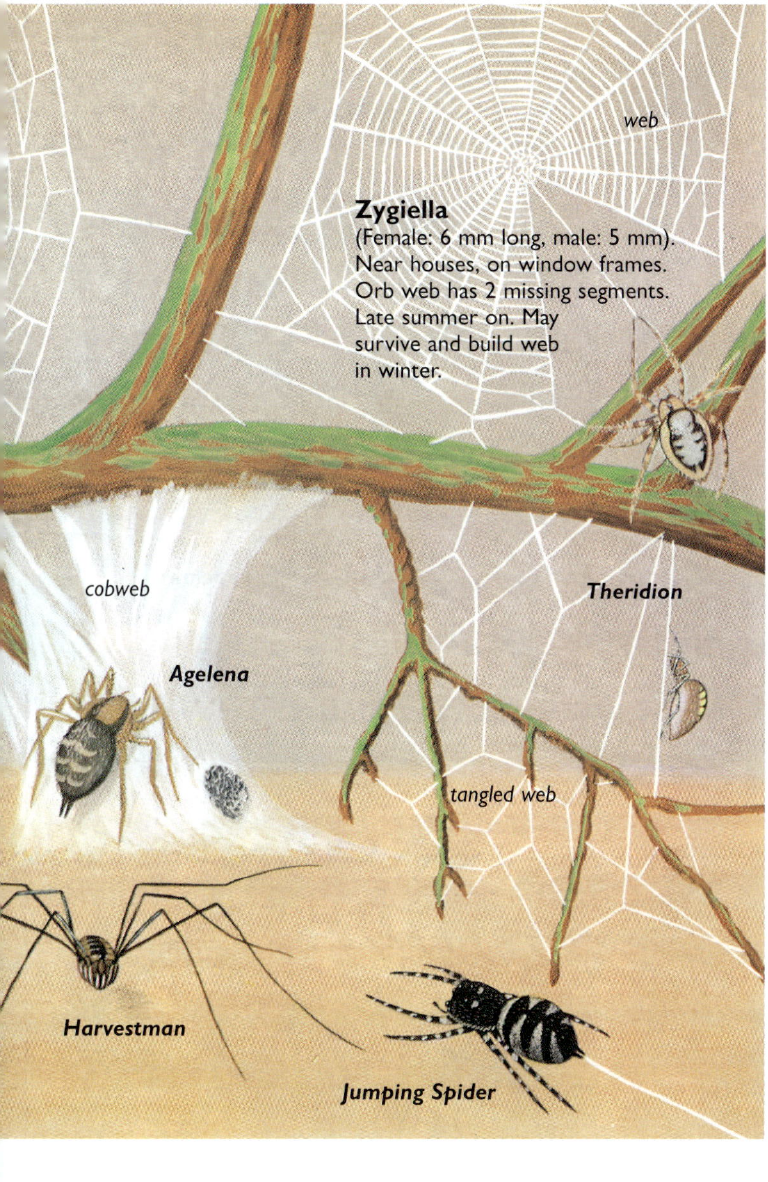

cobweb

Theridion

Agelena

tangled web

Harvestman

Jumping Spider

WOODLICE

Woodlice live under stones and in rotten logs. When frightened some kinds roll themselves up into a ball.

The females carry their eggs and young under their bodies. The young are like their parents and shed their skins as they grow.

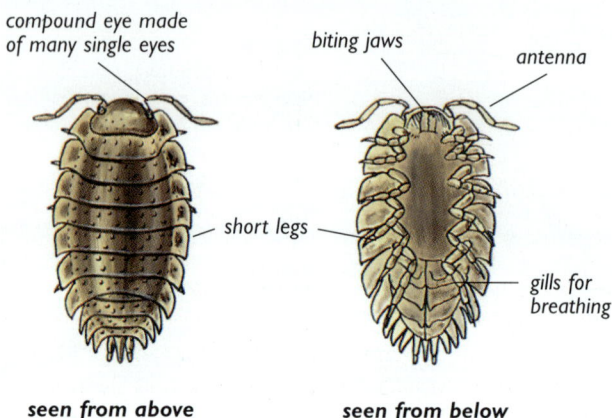

compound eye made of many single eyes

biting jaws

antenna

short legs

gills for breathing

seen from above   **seen from below**

CENTIPEDES

Centipedes are fierce hunting animals. They live in damp, dark places and lay their eggs in the soil. These hatch into young like their parents (see life cycle, page 5).

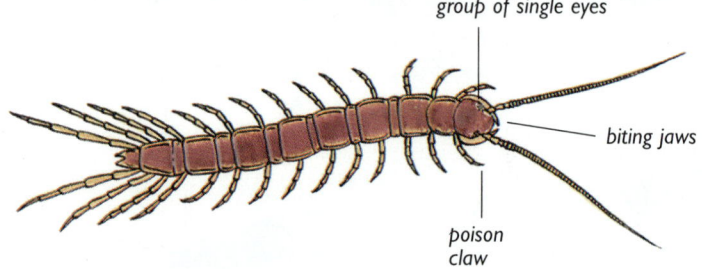

group of single eyes

biting jaws

poison claw

MILLIPEDES

Millipedes nibble plants and are garden pests. They live in damp soil and lay their eggs in small nests of soil. When the young hatch, they have only a very few legs; these grow later and more appear after each moult.

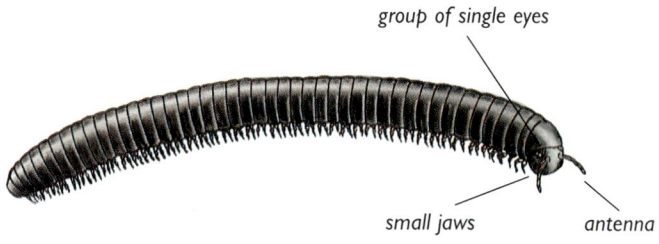

group of single eyes

small jaws   *antenna*

EARTHWORMS

Earthworms live in burrows which they make by pushing and eating the soil away. Some kinds make worm casts from the soil they have eaten; they also pull leaves down into their burrows. They lay eggs in cocoons; these hatch into minute worms like their parents (see life cycle, page 5).

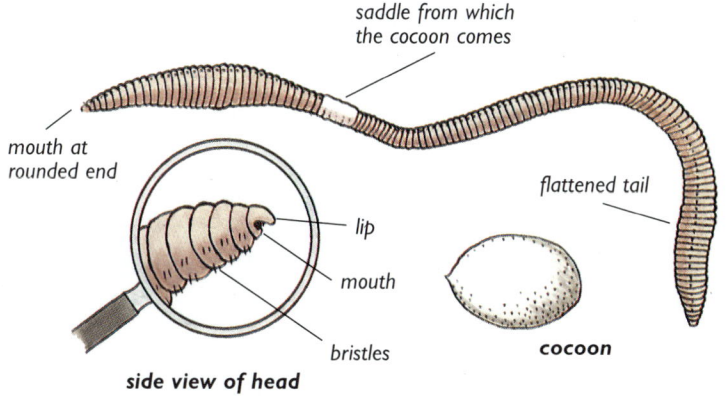

saddle from which the cocoon comes

mouth at rounded end

flattened tail

lip

mouth

bristles

cocoon

side view of head

Woodlouse
(Body 14 mm long).
Damp places. Eats decaying
plant matter.

Pill Woodlouse
(Body 19 mm
long). Drier,
grassy places.
Rolls up when disturbed.

Flat-backed Millipede
(Up to 45 mm long).
In leaf litter and compost.

Pill Millipede
(Up to 25 mm long). Drier places.
Woodlouse-like, but many more
legs. Rolls up when disturbed.

Black Millipede
(Up to 40 mm long). On or in the
soil. Coils when resting.

Spotted Snake Millipede
(Up to 50 mm long).
Cultivated land.
A pest on potatoes.

Centipede
(Up to 60 mm long).
Under stones. Runs fast.

Earthworms
(Up to 300 mm). Burrow
in soil, but emerge on surface
on damp nights.

Whiteworm
(Length 10 mm).
Feeds on decaying
matter in soil.

SNAILS AND SLUGS

Snails and slugs live among plants, under stones or in the soil; they move about when it is damp. The slime trail from the slime gland helps them to cling as they move along using their muscular foot.

They chew plants with their long tongue, called a radula. It is covered with hundreds of teeth.

Snails seal themselves in their shells when the weather is very dry or cold.

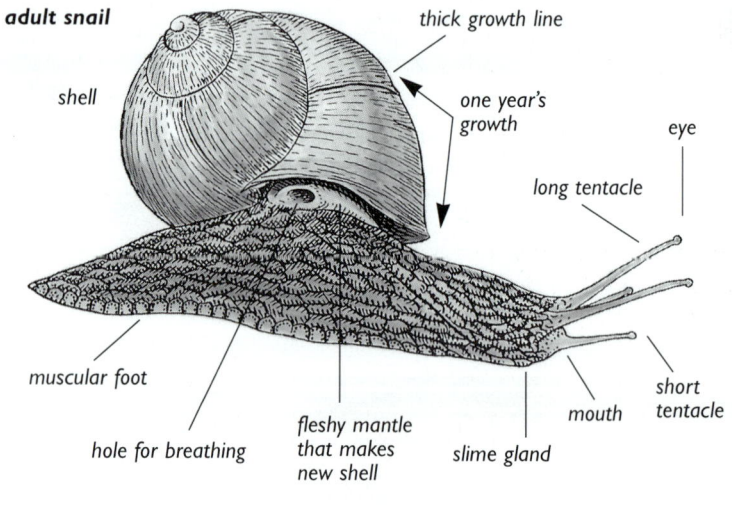

adult snail

shell

thick growth line

one year's growth

eye

long tentacle

muscular foot

hole for breathing

fleshy mantle that makes new shell

slime gland

mouth

short tentacle

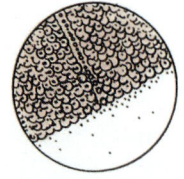

close-up of part of radula of a plant-eating snail

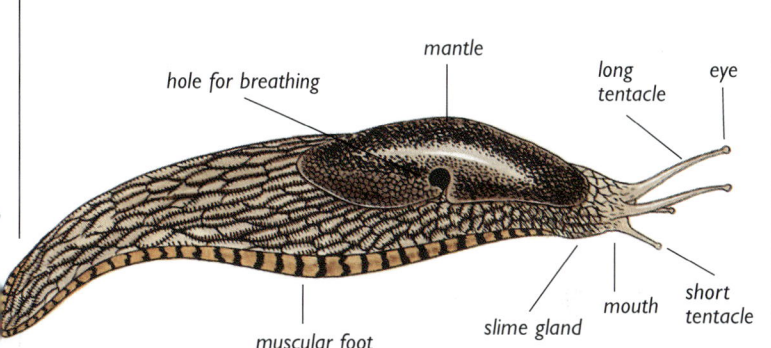

hole for breathing

mantle

long tentacle

eye

muscular foot

slime gland

mouth

short tentacle

adult slug

Snails and slugs both lay eggs in the soil which hatch into tiny animals like their parents (see life cycle, page 5). The shell of the snail gets bigger as the snail grows.

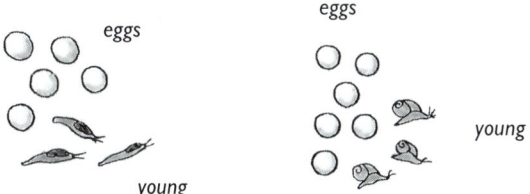

eggs

young

eggs

young

Great Grey Slug
(Up to 200 mm long). Woods, gardens and hedges. Slime colourless, sticky.

Grey Field Slug
(50 mm long). A pest of crops. Slime colourless or white.

Shelled Slug
(Up to 120 mm long). Tiny shell on rear. Feeds on earthworms. Found in parks and gardens.

Black Slug
(Up to 200 mm or more). Often under logs in woods and gardens. Slime colourless.

Pointed Snail
(Shell 15 mm long).
Shaded places, in ground
litter.

Banded Snails
(Shell 25 mm across).
Woods, hedges, grassland and
gardens. Very varied colour
and pattern.

Garden Snail
(Shell 35 mm across).
Widespread, but pest in
gardens.

Roman Snail
(Shell 50 mm across). Woods and
hedges in chalk and limestone areas.
The most important edible snail. In
Britain in south-east only.

Further Reading

Carter, David, *Butterflies and Moths in Britain and Europe*. Pan Books, 1982.
Chinery, Michael, *Collins Guide to the Insects of Britain and Western Europe*. Collins, 1986.
Feltwell, John, *Butterflies and Moths*. Eyewitness Explorer Series, Dorling Kindersley, 1992.
Parker, Steve, *Insects*. Eyewitness Explorer Series, Dorling Kindersley, 1992.
Roberts, Michael, *Collins Guide to the Spiders of Britain and Europe*. Harper Collins, 1995.
Wilkinson, John and Michael Tweedie, *Handy Guide to the Butterflies and Moths of Britain and Europe*. Treasure Press, 1990 (reprint).

A good way to learn more about the animals and plants in your area is to join Wildlife Watch, a club for young people interested in wildlife and the environment. As well as organising activities for its members, Watch produces a national magazine, local newsletters, and many posters and activity packs. Their address is Wildlife Watch, The Green, Witham Park, Waterside South, Lincoln LN5 7JR.